T0069076

David Ippen

The Art of Self

An Interpretation of Traditional Taekwon-Do

Colophon

Hirmer Publishers GmbH
Nymphenburger Straße 84
80636 Munich

Copy-editing, proofreading   Susanna Rachel Michael, New York
Graphic design, typesetting and production   Sabine Frohmader
Lithography   Reproline mediateam, Unterföhring
Printed and bound by   Friedrich Pustet, Regensburg

Printed in Germany

Bibliographic information published by the Deutsche Nationalbibliothek
The Deutsche Nationalbibliothek lists this publication in the Deutsche
Nationalbibliografie; detailed bibliographic data are available on the
Internet at http://dnb.de.

© 2014 Hirmer Publishers GmbH, Munich and the author

ISBN 978-3-7774-2392-0

www.hirmerpublishers.com

Illustration front cover   Famous bamboo grove at Arashiyama, Kyoto, Japan
                                © Fyletto/Bigstock.com
Illustration back cover   © Heather Titus, www.hawaiianlotus.com

David Ippen

The Art of Self

An Interpretation of Traditional Taekwon-Do

HIRMER

Foreword

General Choi Hong Hi, the founder of Taekwon-Do, proclaimed that the main principle of Taekwon-Do is to create a more peaceful world. In this text, I investigate how this claim can be made possible through the study of Taekwon-Do.

The following is a perspective on Taekwon-Do, an interpretation. This is neither a handbook for training nor a manual of technique. Rather, I will be discussing the philosophy of the style of Taekwon-Do that I study. There are other styles, other views on how to interpret Taekwon-Do and its philosophy, and I hope that this book will be seen for what it is: an interpretation of Taekwon-Do from a certain perspective. I respect all styles of Taekwon-Do for putting people in touch with this art and inspiring them to study it. I believe that each student will reap benefits from Taekwon-Do training, no matter which school or style he follows. There is no one absolute truth. Philosophy is the pursuit of wisdom and is understood by studying and questioning a concept or principle. Taekwon-Do, while ostensibly a physical art, is in fact a combination of physical, spiritual, and mental development. This book discusses the philosophy behind the mental and spiritual growth that can develop during the study of Taekwon-Do.

Taekwon-Do needs to be experienced. Daily training is a basic requirement for the committed student, though this book is not about teaching students how to stand, move, block, kick, or punch. There are many books describing all manner of techniques and teaching methods. Instead, this book is meant to increase the awareness of the mental and spiritual aspects of Taekwon-Do training.

It has been said that Taekwon-Do closes the gap between body, mind, and spirit. I do not agree with this statement. There is no gap to close, as they are not separate. There is only a lack of awareness of the interconnectedness of the three. Rather, Taekwon-Do is meant to bring body, mind, and spirit into harmony. But what does this statement mean? How can this be achieved through kicking and punching, push-ups and sit-ups? Very little explanation is given on how such a feat is possible and why we are not already in a state of harmony. We should always question such esoteric claims and reflect on whether or not they hold true for us. I can state that Taekwon-Do has, indeed, done this for me to a certain degree. This book is my explanation of how to bring body, mind, and spirit into harmony through Taekwon-Do; it is meant to showcase how Taekwon-Do can help others to achieve the same thing.

This book interprets Kwon Jae Hwa Taekwon-Do, with no-contact sparring and 20 hyeong. Also known as Traditional Taekwon-Do, it is the style I have trained in for over 25 years. However, many schools that teach Traditional Taekwon-Do have made concessions to modernization and include semi-contact point sparring and four additional hyeong in their curriculum. This book acknowledges the additional four forms to retain the symbolism General Choi intended.

In my years of study I have found many discrepancies between the way this art is taught and the way this art is lived. The words of my teachers did not always match their actions. Their opinions, attitudes, and behaviors outside of the dojang were often hard to justify with the Taekwon-Do philosophy. I learned many different things about the Taekwon-Do philosophy, but trying to make a coherent framework out of it was sometimes difficult, especially in the face of the dissonance between philosophic statements and modeled actions. It seemed that Taekwon-Do philosophy was a very mysterious thing. In this book, I explain Taekwon-Do philosophy as I understand it, hoping to help others to understand it as well. However, living this philosophy can pose a challenge: Taekwon-Do is a way of life and not a sport. In this text, I will discuss this way of life.

I began studying Taekwon-Do in 1990 at the age of 11. Growing up on the outskirts of Munich, I did not have easy access to many martial arts schools at that time. There were Judo and Karate dojos, but no other martial arts that I was aware of. I began to study a bit of Judo and, later, as it became available, Aikido, but they did not satisfy what I was looking for in a martial art. I longed for kicking and punching. After I tried out at the local Taekwon-Do dojang and met the master, I immediately fell in love with this art. It had everything I wanted. Kicks, jumps, hand techniques, breaking of wood, and much more. At the time, I was oblivious to the worldwide magnitude and popularity of Taekwon-Do and the politics surrounding it. My Taekwon-Do world revolved around the dojang where I was studying and my Taekwon-Do teacher. Over time, Taekwon-Do took me around the world to attend many seminars and competitions, and this finally led to the opening of my school in Honolulu, Hawaii on February 9, 2009. Ever since my first day at the Munich dojang, Taekwon-Do has been my passion, and opening a school of my own was the next natural step.

I was fortunate to study Kwon Jae Hwa Taekwon-Do. This style of Taekwon-Do was founded by Grandmaster Kwon Jae Hwa, who introduced Taekwon-Do to Germany in 1965. I attended many seminars under Master Kwon and received personal instruction from him in his dojangs in New York and Portland, Oregon. In 1997 I received my 1st Dan from Master Kwon. He has been a true inspiration to many Taekwon-Do practitioners, beginners and masters alike, in living the life of a master, a teacher, and a pioneer of Taekwon-Do, who has dedicated himself to perpetuating this art. I thank Grandmaster Kwon Jae Hwa for his knowledge, passion, and inspiration, without which I would not have had the opportunity to become a part of this world.

Also, I would like to thank my Kahuna teacher Kahu Abraham Kawaii and his wife Ho'okahi Ho'oulu Hrehorczak-Stephens for their teachings and helping me to understand traditional training and myself. Without them, I would not have ended up in Hawaii. Mahalo Nui Loa.

Lastly, I would like to thank my wife Dr. Andrea Ippen for her support in writing this book.

Author's Note

The reader will note that I exclusively use the male pronoun throughout this text. The reasons for this are twofold: I find the use of "him/her" distracting to the eye, and for many years Taekwon-Do has been a male-dominated art. Fortunately, this trend is changing; at least half of Taekwon-Do practitioners I know are women. I use the male pronoun solely for ease of reading, not to the exclusion or discrimination of women.

Terminology

Dallyon   A dallyon is a freestanding post, usually made of wood, used for conditioning exercises. Practice on a dallyon toughens the arms, hands, legs, and feet, which can help prevent injury to a practitioner in contact situations.

Dobok   The dobok is the uniform worn in Taekwon-Do. "Do" means "the way" and "bok" means "clothing." So it is "clothing in which to study the way." The traditional Taekwon-Do dobok is white and is worn with a colored belt ("tti") around the waist.

Dojang   A Taekwon-Do school or training hall. "Do" means "the way" and "jang" means "a place." So "dojang" literally means "a place in which to study the way." To be more specific, one could say Taekwon-Dojang.

Ha Bog Bu   Located three fingers under the navel, the Ha Bog Bu represents the energetic and spiritual center of the body.

Hangul   The name of the Korean writing system

Hyeong   The Korean term "hyeong" (often romanized as "hyung") means "form" or "pattern." In Taekwon-Do, it refers specifically to a systematic, prearranged sequence of martial techniques that is performed without the use of a weapon. In traditional dojangs, hyeong are used primarily as a form of interval training that is useful in developing mushin, proper kinetics, and mental and physical fortitude. Hyeong can be interpreted as a fight against one or multiple imaginary opponents. Practicing hyeong allows practitioners to perfect their technique without the risk of injuring another person.

Koan   The Chinese word "koan" describes a storied dialogue, a statement, or a question used in Zen Buddhism to assist the student to abandon his ultimate dependence on reason and reach sudden enlightenment.

Mushin   In English, "mushin" would be translated as "no-mind." It is a mental state that the martial artist strives to achieve through his practice. Mushin is the shortened version of "mushin no shin"—"the mind without mind"— a Zen expression that refers to the mind that is not fixed on thought or emotion. Therefore the mind is open to everything. The martial artist seeks to acquire and maintain this state of mushin, not only in his practice, but in his life. The concept of mushin was developed for use on the battlefield to help lead the fighter to victory. If the mind is preoccupied with emotions or thoughts, spontaneous movement cannot happen. The mind should be working at a very high speed and the practitioner should have full awareness of his surroundings; however, it should not be fixed on one thing. Being in a state of mushin allows the practitioner to move freely and respond without conscious thought. The concept of mushin is essential to the practice of martial arts, especially Taekwon-Do. This Zen Buddhist concept is described by the legendary Zen master Takuan Soho:

"The mind must always be in the state of 'flowing,' for when it stops anywhere, that means the flow is interrupted and it is this interruption that is injurious to the well-being of the mind. In the case of the swordsman, it means death. When the swordsman stands against his opponent, he is not to think of the opponent, nor of himself, nor of his enemy's sword movements. He just stands there with his sword which, forgetful of all technique, is ready only to follow the dictates of the subconscious. The man has effaced himself as the wielder of the sword. When he strikes, it is not the man but the sword in the hand of the man's subconscious that strikes." [1]

---

1   Takuan Soho, *The Unfettered Mind*, trans. William Scott Wilson, Tokyo 1986.

Satori "Satori" is a Japanese term used in Zen Buddhism to describe the experience of the awakening or the comprehension of kensho, the true nature of self. In Japanese, "ken" means "self," and "sho" means "nature" or "essence." Usually "satori" is translated into English as "enlightenment." However, to experience satori is only the first step to true enlightenment. The Zen student tries to achieve more frequent moments of satori until it becomes a permanent state leading to Nirvana.

Taekwon-Do-in   Korean for a Taekwon-Do practitioner

Contents

I. What is Taekwon-Do?

Taekwon-Do is a Korean martial art that does not incorporate any weapon practice. Its literal translation is "tae" – foot, "kwon" – hand, "Do" – the way:

The Way of the Hand and Foot

"Tae" refers to all foot techniques, which include kicking, jumping kicks, and blocks. The kicks of Taekwon-Do have become the most widely known aspect of this art. "Kwon" refers to all hand techniques, offensive and defensive. "Do" refers to the spiritual aspect of Taekwon-Do—its philosophy, moral culture, and practice as a way of life. Much of the philosophy and many of the practices and rituals of Taekwon-Do are influenced by Zen Buddhism and the teachings of Confucius and Laozi.

The term "Taekwon-Do" was coined in 1955 by the late Korean General Choi Hong Hi (11/09/1918 – 06/15/2002) along with a panel of Korean martial arts masters who were attempting to find a common term for the martial arts practiced in Korea. General Choi Hong Hi is referred to as the "Father of Taekwon-Do" as he is the founder of this art. General Choi combined techniques from Korean Taekkyon and Shotokan Karate, creating the martial art that became known as "Taekwon-Do."

In 1965, General Choi toured through Egypt, Italy, Malaysia, Singapore, Turkey, and West Germany with a demonstration team in order to introduce and promote Taekwon-Do internationally. Master Kwon Jae Hwa was a member of this demonstration team. In 1966 General Choi founded the International Taekwon-Do Federation (ITF) as the worldwide governing body of Taekwon-Do. After the founding of the ITF, Grandmaster Kwon Jae Hwa separated from General Choi and founded his own system, which he called Traditional Taekwon-Do or Kwon Jae Hwa Taekwon-Do. He brought this system of Taekwon-Do to Germany, where I began my training. These systems are not to be confused with the World Taekwondo Federation (WTF), which was founded in 1973 and is now a recognized Olympic sport.

Traditional Taekwon-Do is the basis for this text, though I believe that the values of this style apply to other styles and systems as well. Traditional Taekwon-Do was taught as a stand-up, no-contact martial art to ensure the practitioners' safety and well-being during partner exercises.

Taekwon-Do is popularly known for its dynamic kicking and jumping techniques. It has gained tremendous popularity because of that, even though it has a good balance of hand and foot techniques. Sometimes the spectacular high-kicking techniques distract the uninitiated from the variety of hand blocks and strikes that Taekwon-Do has to offer. Overall, Taekwon-Do strives to create balance in body, mind, and spirit, and the utilization of the entire body in training is a great tool for achieving just that.

Another very popular aspect of Taekwon-Do is the breaking of material. This demonstrates the force and destructive power behind a strike or kick. However, breaking material (wood, concrete, or stone) is only small fraction of what Taekwon-Do is about. Rather, Taekwon-Do has a profound philosophy and is a way of life, rather than a sport.

Comparable to Karate, Traditional Taekwon-Do follows a ranking system separating student ranks from master ranks. Visually, this is represented by different belt colors. Student ranks are indicated by white, yellow, green, blue, and red belts. A black belt symbolizes the master ranks. The student ranks are called kup or gup, and the master ranks are called dan:

10th & 9th Kup: white belt. The white belt represents the new student. He is the blank canvas that has no knowledge of Taekwon-Do.

8th & 7th Kup: yellow belt. The yellow belt represents the seed of knowledge that is planted in the ground.

6th & 5th Kup: green belt. The green belt symbolizes the plant of knowledge that is growing into a tree.

4th & 3rd Kup: blue belt. The blue belt represents the sky that the tree has reached; it stands for limitless options.

2nd & 1st Kup: red belt. The red belt symbolizes danger; something important is about to occur.

1st Dan – 9th Dan: black belt. The black belt represents a combination of all colors. It encompasses all the other colors and their knowledge. It is also the color of the universe and its vast expanses.

Depending on the style of Taekwon-Do, the title "master" is awarded at 3rd, 4th or 5th Dan, and "grandmaster" at 5th or 7th Dan. In Traditional Taekwon-Do, those who achieve 5th Dan or higher are considered to be grandmasters. 9th Dan represents the highest possible rank in Taekwon-Do and has a special position as it is supposed to be reserved for the leader of the entire art, both in technique and spirit.

All students are required to wear a white uniform; the white dobok symbolizes purity of mind and hints at the core philosophy of using Taekwon-Do to promote peace. All accessories and makeup should be removed before entering the dojang. It also reduces us to what are at our core: human beings, without accouterments. In the dojang, all students assemble to practice Do together, and the white uniform represents unity in pursuing the spirit of the Do of Taekwon. Only black belts are allowed to wear a uniform with black trim on the dobok top, which represents their rank and seniority. Before entering the dojang, the feet should be washed and a clean dobok should be put on. This constitutes a cleansing ritual to make us aware of our purpose in the space and to separate between the dojang and the world outside.

II. The Three Parts of Traditional Taekwon-Do

Traditional Taekwon-Do can be divided into the three basic parts of physical training:

1. Hyeong (Forms)
2. Taeryon (Sparring)
3. Kyek Pa (Breaking)

These represent the most basic aspects of training in this art. Each one has its own importance and value.

1. Hyeong

Hyeong is a vital, if not the essential, part of Taekwon-Do. Initially, there were 20 hyeong; General Choi later added four more to complete his system. The 24 patterns represent 24 hours—one day. Over time, days accumulate to encompass the entire span of one's life.

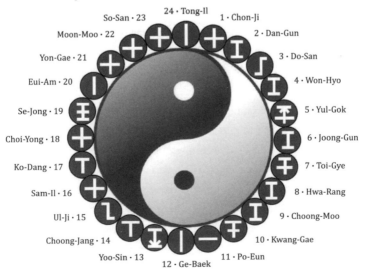

Hyeong form the technical foundation of this art. It is crucial to understand them well and know their applications. Through hyeong, the art is perpetuated because they represent a compilation of the movements of Taekwon-Do. With knowledge of all hyeong, a practitioner knows the basics of the complete Taekwon-Do system. Properly understood, hyeong offer limitless options of recombining their individual techniques. Furthermore, the core philosophic principle of Taekwon-Do—that it only be used for defensive purposes—is symbolized in all hyeong as each one begins with a defensive movement.

1.1 Technical Understanding and Application of Hyeong

Hyeong are symbolic fights against one or more imaginary opponents. The various hyeong were created so that the practitioner could practice his technique at full strength without ever endangering, hurting, or even confronting another person. Hyeong provide physical, mental, and spiritual practice. They strengthen the body, increase agility, speed, and stamina, and can be used as a tool for recovery after disease or injury as low-impact training. Proper understanding of the forms and the ability to deconstruct and reconstruct movement patterns from hyeong provide a practitioner with the ability to create unlimited combinations of movement. This is essential to advanced training, as students are sometimes in situations in which they are not able to attend classes at a dojang. So hyeong, once mastered and understood, eventually become a tool for the individual to continue his training without supervision.

Proper breathing technique plays a vital role in all Taekwon-Do movements but is particularly important in hyeong. Breath control involves intake through the nose and exhalation through the mouth. During exhalation, the yell of "Kiap" is used when impacting a surface in order to assist with the generation of more force. Breathing is centered in the Ha Bog Bu, located three fingers under the navel. This is where the "Kiap" should come from as well. The Ha Bog Bu represents the energetic and spiritual center of the body. This is also where the belt knot is worn, to make the practitioner aware of where his focus should be centered, where all power for movement should be generated from, and where his breathing should be focused.

The shout of "Kiap" focuses and increases the amount of force that is generated within a technique. It also can intimidate an attacker, acting as a deterrent. Much like exhaling when lifting a heavy object, "Kiap" prevents over-pressurization of the lungs during strenuous movements; this reduces the risk of rupturing the alveoli. With "Kiap," the student learns proper breath control. In Traditional Taekwon-Do, the practitioner does not exhale after every movement. This facilitates a more dynamic and natural interpretation of hyeong in terms of the flow of movement. "Kiap" is used at certain times during hyeong to express strong attacks or blocks. Through breath training, the practitioner learns to control his breath at all times and not to reveal breathing patterns to opponents. During or after physical strain, breath control should be regained as quickly as possible. In Taekwon-Do, we try to conceal breathing patterns to not show exhaustion, as this knowledge would give an advantage to an opponent. An opponent might anticipate the relaxation of the abdomen during exhalation and use this as an opportunity to attack. "Kiap" should be the only audible exhalation; the forced exhalation with "Kiap" tightens the abdominal muscles and acts as a protective shield for impact. In general, the Taekwon-Do practitioner should strive to not show his emotional or physical states during Taekwon-Do. Allowing an opponent to read one's mental or physical state can be a huge disadvantage in sparring matches.

On a physiological level, holding the breath for a few seconds at a time will increase oxygen assimilation and prevent hyperventilation. In order to build greater stamina, breath and movement have to become one. The individual rhythm of the hyeong has to be realized, and only through training can breath be properly matched to the hyeong. To understand this rhythm, the individual movements require a certain amount of refinement. Any unnecessary movement should be eliminated from a technique to allow proper functioning and execution. The correct execution of technique requires the full focus of the practitioner, both mentally and physically. Body, mind, and spirit should all be engaged in movement, thus unlocking the maximum potential of any given technique. Through hyeong, at first with guided instruction and later through self-correction, a practitioner learns to align and engage his entire being to facilitate action. Extraordinary physical feats are possible once the body is correctly aligned and moves in harmony with mind and spirit.

This transcends mere muscle memory and automated repetition of learned movement patterns, as it requires the ability to visualize various attacks and respond to them with a set pattern of movements. Further, hyeong can be practiced without any outward movement, through the visualization of attacks and defense. This corresponds to modern visualization training techniques used by athletes to increase the retention of learned movement patterns and their refined execution. Modern neuroscience has shown that thinking about a movement activates the same areas in the brain as actually performing the movement, though with a lower rate of neuron activity.

In terms of our conscious thought processes, training hyeong sharpens the mind and increases the ability to analyze a situation from different angles. To know both the attack and the defense of the movements in each hyeong means to understand the mindset of both attacker and defender. It increases complex-problem-solving abilities—in this case, defending against an attack. Hyeong is not just about knowing the movements and internalizing them, but also understanding their purpose and being able to respond appropriately.

This practice creates internal completion and a connection between both sides: attacker and defender. When properly understood, the practitioner realizes that they are one and the same. The practice of attaining this unison in the technical understanding of hyeong is represented in the Daoist symbol of the yin-yang. Only the balance between both parts—attacker and defender—will create harmony in hyeong and within oneself. The same applies to all aspects of Taekwon-Do and to all aspects of life, as well.

In addition, all hyeong should start and end in the same spot, representing the idea of completion and, moreover, the entire circle of life. This also brings us back to the symbolism of the yin-yang; not the dualism of the drops within it, but the circle surrounding it. It touches on the concept of karma and the inevitability of death. Hyeong represent the struggle of life and the achievements of one's lifespan. In the end, the practitioner always returns to where he came from, having performed at his highest level of capability during the process. Hyeong stand for the choices one makes and the impact one can create in life. Through refining technique, a practitioner is able to create change and engender evolution within himself.

For the beginning student, the focus of practicing hyeong lies on learning the right sequence of the individual techniques and their proper execution. The previously discussed aspects of hyeong are seldom consciously grasped. Though he is not aware of or able to intellectualize the symbolism inherent in hyeong, the student still receives the benefits of this training. Over time, he will integrate the mental and spiritual aspects alongside the physical. Beyond all technical application, hyeong create unison between body, mind, and spirit.

1.2 Symbolic Meaning of Hyeong

In addition to the proper understanding of each of the movements in hyeong, the student learns their symbolic meanings. Each hyeong represents an important historic event or person in Korean history. Many of the hyeong are named after heroic figures from the Three Kingdoms period (57 B.C.E. – 668 C.E.), which consisted of the kingdoms of Baekje, Goguryeo, and Silla. In hyeong, the diagrams, number of movements, movement sequences, and choice of particular movements all carry meaning and add to the significance of each hyeong. The following brief descriptions illustrate the Traditional Taekwon-Do hyeong.

1. Chon-Ji (19 movements):
"Chon-Ji" literally means "Heaven and Earth." It is interpreted as the creation of the world or the beginning of human history; therefore, it is the initial pattern learned by the beginner. This pattern consists of two similar parts, one to represent Heaven (middle outside forearm block) and the other the Earth (downward outside forearm block). The symbolism of the two parts of this hyeong represents the creation of the dualistic universe through the movement of yin-yang. Its diagram (+) also addresses all four cardinal directions equally. The symbolism of this hyeong hints at

the symbolism of the South Korean national flag (Taegukki). This pattern with its basic movements and stances constitutes the foundation for understanding the other 23 hyeong.

2. Dan-Gun (21 movements):

This hyeong is named after the holy Dan-Gun Wanggeom, the legendary founder of Gojoseon, the first Korean kingdom. Emperor Dan-Gun's reign is calculated to have begun in 2333 B.C.E. He was said to have been the son of a bear that became a woman through the grace of the gods. He located his capital city of Asadal on a mountain; all punches in this hyeong aim high, referring to Dan-Gun scaling a mountain.

3. Do-San (24 movements):

Do-San, or Tosan, is the pen name of the patriot Ahn Ch'ang-Ho (1876 – 1938 C.E.), who was a Korean independence activist and one of the early leaders of the Korean-American immigrant community. Ahn and his wife moved to the U.S. in 1902 to further his education. During his stay in the U.S., he was very active in the Korean community and founded two organizations: the Friendship Society in 1903 and the Mutual Assistance Society in 1906. However, Ahn's main concern was the reform of the Korean peoples' character and the social system in Korea, primarily through educational reform and the modernization of schools. Upon his return to Korea in 1907, he founded the Shinminhoe (New Korea Society), which was the most important organization to fight the Japanese occupation. Ahn was arrested by the Japanese more than five times for his patriotism and activism in the Korean independence movement. Do-San hyeong honors his commitment to the Korean people.

4. Won-Hyo (28 movements):

This hyeong is named after the monk Won-Hyo (617 – 686 C.E.), who was one of the leading thinkers, writers, and commentators of the Korean

Buddhist tradition. He wrote over 80 books of commentaries on the most influential Mahayana scriptures. He was famous for singing and dancing in the streets and, even though the Buddha discourages such behavior, his songs were seen as a means to save all sentient beings. His life spanned the end of the Three Kingdoms period of Korea, and he was instrumental in spreading Buddhism in the newly formed kingdom of Silla.

He began teaching after an experience revealed to him the power of the human mind. While he was a monk, he and a close friend were traveling to China for further study. During the journey, heavy rains forced them to take shelter, which they did in what they believed to be an earthen sanctuary. In the night, Won-Hyo became incredibly thirsty and sought water. In the darkness, he found what he thought was a gourd filled with drinking water. A long draught of the refreshing water satiated his thirst, and he was able to sleep. Upon waking, however, the companions found themselves in an ancient tomb. What Won-Hyo had thought was a gourd filled with fresh water was, in fact, a human skull, and the water inside was brackish and undrinkable. Amazed at the power of the human mind to transform reality, he left the priesthood to share his "consciousness-only" enlightenment experience and spread the word of the Buddhadharma. From this experience and his subsequent teachings, Won-Hyo became a popular folk hero in Korean culture.

5. Yul-Gok (38 movements):

Yul-Gok is the pen name of the great philosopher and scholar Yi I (1536 – 1584 C.E.), who was nicknamed the "Confucius of Korea." The 38 movements of this pattern refer to his birthplace on the 38° latitude, and the diagram represents the Hangul for "scholar." Yi I was an active government official who served in various positions. He was not only a philosopher, but also a reformer who thought it important to implement Confucian values and principles in government administration. He emphasized sage learning and self-cultivation as the basis of proper administration. This follows the Confucian principle that if you want to govern others, you have to first learn to govern yourself. Yi I's picture can be found on the current 5,000 won note in South Korea.

6. Joong-Gun (32 movements):

This hyeong is named after the patriot An Joong-Gun, who assassinated Ito Hirobumi, the first Japanese prime minister and the first governor-general of Korea. Ito Hirobumi played the leading part in what later became Japan's annexation of Korea. An shot Ito following the signing of the Eulsa Treaty in 1905 C.E. This treaty deprived Korea of its diplomatic sovereignty and made Korea a protectorate of Japan. At his trial, An listed 15 "charges" in justification of the killing of Ito:

1. Assassination of the Korean Empress Myeongseong
2. Dethroning of Emperor Gojong
3. Forcing of 14 unequal treaties on Korea
4. Massacre of innocent Koreans
5. Usurpation of the authority of the Korean government by force
6. Plundering of Korean railroads, mines, forests, and rivers
7. Imposition of the use of Japanese banknotes
8. Disbanding of the Korean armed forces
9. Obstruction of the education of Koreans
10. Banning Koreans from studying abroad
11. Confiscation and burning of Korean textbooks
12. Spreading a rumor around the world that Koreans wanted Japanese protection
13. Deception of the Japanese Emperor by saying that the relationship between Korea and Japan was peaceful when in truth it was full of hostility and conflicts
14. Breaking the peace of Asia
15. Assassination of Emperor Komei

"I killed Ito Hirobumi because he disturbed the peace of the Orient and estranged the relationship between Korea and Japan. I hope that if Korea and Japan are friendlier and are ruled peacefully, they would be a model all throughout the five continents. I did not kill Ito misunderstanding his intentions." – An Joong-Gun.

Joong-Gun hyeong has 32 movements to represent An's age when he was executed in prison in 1910.

7. Toi-Gye (37 movements):

Toi-Gye is the penname of the noted scholar Yi Hwang (1501 – 1570 C.E.), one of the two authorities on Neo-Confucianism during the Joseon dynasty. The other was his younger contemporary, Yi I (Yul-Gok). Yi Hwang established both the Yeongnam School and the Dosan Seowon, a private Confucian academy. During his lifetime, Yi held several government positions and was involved in the purging of corrupt government officials. Yi was known for his integrity, and on numerous occasions he was even exiled from the capital for his firm commitment to his principles. In his forty years of public service, he served four kings—Jungjong, Injong, Myeongjong, and Seonjo—and was brought back from retirement several times at the request of the kings. Yi Hwang's picture is on the current 1,000 won note in South Korea. Taekwon-Do honors Yi Hwang's name with Toi-Gye hyeong; the 37 movements of the pattern refer to his birthplace on the 37° latitude, and the diagram symbolizes "scholar."

8. Hwa-Rang (29 movements):

Hwa-Rang hyeong is named after the Hwa-Rang youth group, which originated in the Silla dynasty in the 5th century C.E. The Hwa-Rang was an elite group that trained in various arts, including horsemanship, swordsmanship, archery, javelin and stone throwing, polo, and ladder-climbing. In addition to physical training, the Hwa-Rang members were greatly influenced by Buddhist, Confucian, and Taoist ideals and studied poetry, song, and dance. By the 7th century, the organization had grown in prestige and numbered several hundred bands. This group eventually became the driving force for the unification of the three kingdoms of

Korea, though there is historical debate about the actual function of the Hwa-Rang as the organization was originally not military in character.

The 29 movements of this hyeong stand for the 29th Infantry Division, where Taekwon-Do was mainly developed under General Choi Hong Hi.

9. Choong-Moo (30 movements):

Choong-Moo was the honorary name given to the great Admiral Yi Sun-Sin of the Joeseon dynasty. One of Yi's greatest accomplishments was resurrecting and improving the turtle ship (kobukson), which was the precursor to the present-day submarine, in 1592 C.E. The ship was heavily armored and the roof was covered with planks and spikes. The purpose of the spikes was to prevent the ship from being boarded by the enemy; the larger Japanese ships' sides were higher than those of the turtle ships, and thus the spikes prevented boarders from jumping down onto the roof without risking impalement. Japanese naval strategy relied heavily on boarding enemy ships and defeating them in hand-to-hand combat, which the turtle ships made impossible. Additionally, Yi personally ensured that cannon technology was developed to give the Korean fleet an advantage in battle. Admiral Yi repulsed several Japanese invasions between 1592 and 1598 and was never defeated, though historians have discovered that he was involved in at least 23 battles.

Perhaps his greatest victory was the battle of Myeongnyang, when Yi's 13 battleships were outnumbered by approximately 333 Japanese ships. Yi lured the Japanese fleet into the Myeongnyang Strait, which had powerful currents, limiting safe entrance to only one ship at a time. The Japanese were unfamiliar with the strait, and on that day there was a heavy mist that decreased visibility. In addition, Yi had iron chains spanning the entire width of the strait to hinder the Japanese ships' movements. This way, the Japanese fleet could not use their numerical advantage to envelope the Korean ships. In the end, after many Japanese ships had been destroyed, the Japanese fleet pulled back. This victory turned the tide of the entire war against the Japanese; their ground forces on the verge of invading Hanseong were cut off from a steady flow of supplies and reinforcements, and were forced to retreat.

Yi died on the battlefield from a single bullet wound at the battle of Noryang on December 16, 1598. Due to plotting and framing by his rivals and Japanese spies, Admiral Yi was stripped of his rank and tortured several times in his life on the orders of King Seonjo. Today, Admiral Yi is considered one of Korea's greatest heroes of all time. Koreans look upon Yi as a man of courage, perseverance, strength, self-sacrifice, intellect, and loyalty to his country.

The hyeong honoring Admiral Yi ends with a left-hand attack to symbolize the tragedy of his death, which occurred before he could be fully acknowledged for his potential and achievements, and because of his unreserved loyalty to the king.

10. Kwang-Gae (39 movements):
Kwang-Gae hyeong is named after the famous Gwanggaeto Wang (374 – 413 C.E.), the 19th king of the Goguryeo dynasty. Under Gwanggaeto, the kingdom of Goguryeo once again became a major power of East Asia, previously having enjoyed this status in the 2nd century C.E. Upon Gwanggaeto's death at thirty-nine years of age, Goguryeo controlled all territories between the Amur and Han rivers (this consisted of two-thirds of modern Korea, Manchuria, parts of Russia's Primorsky Krai, and Inner Mongolia). The diagram of this hyeong represents the expansion and recovery of territory. In addition to conquering new territories, Gwanggaeto captured Baekje's capital in present-day Seoul and made Baekje its vassal. This occurred after Silla, in 399, submitted to Goguryeo for protection from raids by Baekje. Many consider this loose unification under Goguryeo to have been the only true unification of the three kingdoms. The 39 movements of this pattern refer to first two figures of 391, the year he came to the throne, and his 39 years of age at his death.

11. Po-Eun (36 movements):

Po-Eun is the penname of Jeong Mongju (1337 – 1392 C.E.), who was a Korean civil minister and scholar during the late period of the Goryeo dynasty. In 1367 he became an instructor in Neo-Confucianism at the Gukjagam, then called Seonggyungwan, while simultaneously holding a government position. Jeong was a faithful public servant to King U (1365 – 1389 C.E.) and the king had great confidence in Jeong's wide range of knowledge and good judgment.

Jeong was murdered in 1392 on the Sonjukkyo Bridge in Gaeseong following a banquet held for him by Yi Bangwon (later Taejong of Joseon), the fifth son of Yi Seonggye. Yi Seonggye overthrew the Goryeo dynasty in order to found the Joseon dynasty. Jeong was murdered because he refused to betray his loyalty to the Goryeo dynasty. Yi Bangwon recited a poem to dissuade Jeong from remaining loyal to the Goryeo court:

"What if one goes this way, or that way?
What if arrowroots of Mt. Mansu be tangled together?
Tangled likewise, let us prosper for a hundred years."

But Jeong answered with another poem that affirmed his loyalty:

"Though I die and die again a hundred times,
That my bones turn to dust, whether my soul remains or not,
Ever loyal to my Lord, how can this red heart ever fade away?"

The diagram of this hyeong, a straight line (-), symbolizes Jeong's unerring loyalty to his king and country. It is also a reference to the bridge on which Jeong was murdered.

12. Ge-Baek (44 movements):

This hyeong is named after General Ge-Baek (? – 660 C.E.) of the Baekje kingdom in ancient Korea. Ge-Baek was known for his military discipline, honor, and bravery. He was killed in the Battle of Hwangsanbeol

(660 C.E.) by Silla forces under General Kim Yoo-Sin and his allies from the Chinese Tang dynasty. Ge-Baek commanded only 5,000 troops in this battle against 50,000 Silla troops. Ge-Baek was able to repulse the Silla forces five times before his troops were defeated. The Battle of Hwang-sanbeol was the last stand of the Baekje kingdom against the Silla, and Ge-Baek's defeat marked the end of the Baekje kingdom. King Uija of the Baekje kingdom surrendered shortly after Ge-Baek's death. The diagram of Gye-Baek hyeong (I) represents his severe and strict military discipline.

13. *Yoo-Sin (68 movements):*

Yoo-Sin hyeong is named after Kim Yoo-Sin, the great general of the Silla dynasty who was instrumental in uniting the three kingdoms of Korea. The 68 movements of this pattern refer to the last two figures of the year 668 C.E., the year of the unification of the whole of Korea. The ready posture signifies a sword drawn on the right rather than the left side, symbolizing Kim's mistake of following his king's orders to fight with Chinese forces against his own nation. With the help of the Silla navy and some 130,000 Tang forces, Kim attacked the Baekje capital, Sabi, in 660. The Battle of Hwangsanbeol is one of the most famous battles of the 7th century. In this battle, he killed general Ge-Baek of Baekje and conquered that kingdom. After a failed attempt in 661, Kim successfully attacked and defeated the kingdom of Goguryeo in 668, thus uniting the three kingdoms into one. This marked the beginning of the division between North and South Korea, with the unified Silla dynasty (669 – 935 C.E.) to the south and the Balhae dynasty (698 – 926 C.E.) to the north.

14. *Choong-Jang (52 movements):*

Choong Jang was the given name of the 16th-century General Kim Dok-Ryong of the Yi dynasty. Despite his small stature, Kim was known for his agility, bravery, and outstanding ability in battle. Kim and his brother, Kim Duk-Hong, joined the military in 1592 C.E. when the Japanese invaded Korea under Hideyoshi Toyotomi (Imjin War). Kim's brother was killed during this war, but he remained in the military and proved his skill multiple times in battle against the Japanese invaders. In 1594 Kim was appointed royal messenger and given the name General Yikho by King Seonjo.

In 1596 Yi Mong-Hak started a rebellion in Jeolla province and General Kim was sent to quell it. When Kim found out that the leader, Yi Mong-Hak, had died, he retreated with his troops. However, Kim was accused of being part of this rebellion by jealous subordinates of the king, and was arrested. Kim was subsequently executed based on these false charges; he was 29 years old. This particular pattern ends with a left hand attack, which signifies that he died in prison on a false charge at a young age, preventing him from demonstrating his full capabilities.

Sixty-five years after his death, after it was revealed that the charges were based on false testimonies, General Kim was exonerated and his government position restored to him. In 1681, General Kim was post-humously awarded the title of Minister of War for his bravery and loyalty. Several other posthumous titles were bestowed upon General Kim and a shrine was built in his memory.

15. Ul-Ji (42 movements):

Ul-Ji hyeong is named after the great General Ul-Ji Mun-Dok (also Eulji-Mundeok or Ulchi Mundok) of the Goguryeo dynasty in the 7th century C.E. The diagram of this hyeong reflects his surname. Ul-Ji successfully defended Goguryeo from the Chinese Sui invasion in 612 C.E. The Sui vastly outnumbered the Goguryeo forces, but Ul-Ji limited their forces by fighting only small engagements at times and places of his choosing. These engagements led the Chinese troops further and further from their supply centers, weakening the Sui forces. Meanwhile, the Sui sent an advance battalion to take the city of Pyongyang, where Ul-Ji ultimately defeated the Chinese in the Battle of Salsu. This battle came to be known as one of the most glorious military triumphs in Korea's national history. With this victory, Ul-Ji was able to hold the Chinese invasion forces back long enough for winter to set in; the troops had to return home as they were short on provisions and could not outlast a winter siege. Ul-Ji is considered one of Korea's greatest military generals and historic figures. Today, a main thoroughfare in downtown Seoul, Euljiro, is named after him. Also, the second-highest military decoration of South Korea, Field Marshal Lord Eulji's Order of Military Merit, is named in his honor.

16. Sam-Il (33 movements):

This hyeong refers to the Sam-Il movement of 1919 C.E. (Literally, the "three-one" movement, or "March 1st" movement), which was one of the earliest public displays of Korean resistance during the occupation of Korea by the Japanese Empire. The Sam-Il movement was a response to Japanese oppression and was triggered by the Fourteen Points outlining the right of national "self-determination" proclaimed by U.S. President Woodrow Wilson at the Paris Peace Conference in January 1919.

At 2:00 P.M. on March 1, 1919, 33 activists who formed the core of the Sam-Il movement convened at Taehwagwan Restaurant in Seoul and read the Korean Declaration of Independence that had been drawn up by historian Choe Nam-Seon. The leaders of the movement signed the document and sent a copy to the Governor General. The declaration read:

"We herewith proclaim the independence of Korea and the liberty of the Korean people. This we proclaim to all the nations of the world in witness of human equality. This we proclaim to our descendants so that they may enjoy in perpetuity their inherent right to nationhood. Inasmuch as this proclamation originates from our five-thousand-year history, inasmuch as it springs from the loyalty of twenty million people, inasmuch as it affirms our yearning for the advancement of everlasting liberty, inasmuch as it expresses our desire to take part in the global reform rooted in human conscience, it is the solemn will of heaven, the great tide of our age, and a just act necessary for the co-existence of all humankind. Therefore, no power in this world can obstruct or suppress it!"

After the signing, the members of the Sam-Il movement called the police and informed them of their actions. They were subsequently arrested. Many delegates associated with the movement read copies of the declaration in public, causing huge crowds to gather in peaceful processions. Eventually, these processions grew so large that the Japanese police were not able to suppress the crowds; they called for military and naval support. The processions turned violent, causing many arrests, injuries, and casualties in the Korean populace.

The Sam-Il movement served as a catalyst for the Korean independence movement and led to the establishment the Provisional Government of the Republic of Korea in Shanghai in April 1919. In the aftermath of the Sam-Il movement, activists in the Korean independence movement were hunted down by the Japanese government. Many Korean independence leaders expatriated to Manchuria, Shanghai, and other parts of China, where they continued their activities.

On May 24, 1949, March 1 was designated as a national holiday in South Korea. The 33 movements of Sam-Il hyeong stand for the 33 patriots who planned the independence movement.

17. Ko-Dang (39 movements):

Ko-Dang is the pseudonym of the patriot Cho Man-Sik, who dedicated his life to the independence movement and education of Korea. Cho was a nationalist activist in Korea's independence movement during the Japanese occupation that ended in 1945 C.E. He was also involved in the March 1st movement (Sam-Il movement) in 1919, and openly opposed Japanese occupation. However, he followed a policy of strictly non-violent resistance and led through example, earning him the name "Gandhi of Korea." Throughout his life, he was imprisoned nearly forty times for his activism. In addition to his efforts opposing the Japanese, Cho promoted Korean economic self-sufficiency and established the Korean Products Promotion Society in 1922, with the objective that Koreans obtain solely home-produced products. After World War II, Cho became involved in the power struggle that enveloped North Korea in the months following

Japan's surrender. Due to his popularity, Cho was initially supported by the Soviet Union to rule North Korea. However, due to his opposition to the proposed trusteeship of North Korea by the Soviet Union, Cho lost Soviet support and was forced from power by the Soviet-backed communists in the north. Cho was placed under house arrest in January 1946, where he continued to vocally oppose communism. Cho later disappeared into the North Korean prison system, where he was supposedly executed in 1950.

The 39 movements of Ko-Dang hyeong show the number of times he was imprisoned as well as the location of his birthplace on the 39° latitude.

18. Choi-Yong (45 movements):

This hyeong is named after the famous General Choi-Yong (also Choi Young, and romanized as Choe Yeong) (1316 – 1388 C.E.), who was the premier and commander in chief of the armed forces toward the end of Goryeo dynasty (14th century). Even though Choi had been born into a relatively wealthy family, his beginnings were humble and his lifestyle was modest. He cared little for expensive clothes or meals, and disliked men who desired expensive articles. Choi viewed simplicity as a virtue. His motto, taught to him by his father, was "Do not be covetous of gold."

Choi chose a military career and quickly gained the confidence of both his men and his king during numerous battles with Japanese pirates who began raiding the Korean coast around 1350. At the age of 36, Choi became a national hero when he successfully put down a rebellion by Jo Il-Shin, who had surrounded the palace with sympathetic troops and had himself declared king. As the Goryeo kingdom had been a dependency of China's Yuan dynasty since the 13th century, Choi-Yong also assisted the Yuan dynasty in many victorious battles. Additionally, he re-conquered some of the northern territories west of the Yalu River that had been previously lost to the Mongols.

In 1388, Choi-Yong was executed on a false charge made by one of his subordinate commanders, General Yi Song-Gye. Yi later became the first king of the Yi dynasty. During what came to be known as the Wihwado Retreat, Yi had used his popularity with high-ranking government officials and the general populace to stage a coup d'état. Choi-Yong bravely fought Yi at the palace, but was eventually overwhelmed by Yi's forces. After his defeat, Choi was exiled and later executed. During his life, Choi-Yong was very popular and greatly respected by all nations for his loyalty, patriotism, and honest modesty.

19. Se-Jong (24 movements):
Se-Jong is named after King Se-Jong the Great (1397 – 1450 C.E.), who invented the Korean writing system, Hangul, in the year 1443. This allowed all classes of society to become literate. Before the invention of Hangul, only the upper classes and nobility were able to read and write as Korean was written in Chinese characters, and learning them was a very difficult and exclusive matter. There was some resistance to Hangul from the upper classes, but Hangul took root and greatly furthered the overall education of the Korean people.

During his reign, King Se-Jong implemented many changes to bring prosperity to Korea. He ordered the compilation of a farmer's handbook to assist farmers in acquiring and implementing farming techniques. He encouraged people to behave according to Confucianism, thus making it a social norm. King Se-Jong was also a strong supporter of science; he ordered his astronomers to create a calendar with the Korean capital of Seoul determining the Primary Meridian, thereby allowing them to accurately predict lunar and solar eclipses. He also furthered cannon development and strengthened other areas of the military. King Se-Jong is one of the two kings in Korean history who were posthumously awarded the title "the Great," the other king being King Gwanggaeto. The diagram of this hyeong dedicated to Se-Jong represents "king," and the 24 movements refer to the 24 letters of the Korean alphabet.

20. (24) Tong-Il (56 movements):

Tong-Il denotes the unification of Korea, which has been divided into two separate states. The diagram of Tong-Il hyeong symbolizes the unity of the Korean people. The division of Korea stems from the victory of the Allied forces in World War II over the Japanese Empire, which ended the Japanese Empire's 35-year colonial rule of Korea. The U.S. and the Soviet Union initially agreed to temporarily occupy the country as a trustee-ship, with the U.S. in the south of the Korean peninsula and the Soviet Union in the north. The 38th parallel was set as the border separating the two zones. The purpose of this trusteeship was to establish a Korean provisional government, which would, in due course, become free and independent. However, the U.S. and Soviet Union backed different leaders and, in 1948, two states were effectively established, each of which claimed sovereignty over the whole Korean peninsula. The friction between the two Korean states—the Democratic People's Republic of Korea in the north, and the Republic of Korea in the south—and raids and skirmishes along the border led to the Korean War (1950 – 1953). This left the two Koreas separated by the Korean Demilitarized Zone on the 38th parallel. To this day, Korea remains separated and tension between the states remains. Tong-Il hyeong stands for the hope of the reunification of the two Koreas.

The additional four hyeong (now numbered 20-23) are as follows:

– *Eui-Am (45 movements):*

Eui-Am is the pseudonym of Son Byong Hi, the leader of the Korean in-dependence movement of March 1, 1919 (the Sam-Il movement). The 45 movements of this hyeong refer to his age when he changed the name of Donghak ("Eastern Learning") to Chondo Kyo ("Heavenly Way Religion") in 1905. The diagram represents his indomitable spirit, displayed while dedicating himself to the prosperity of his nation.

Donghak was an academic movement in Korean Neo-Confucian-ism founded in 1860 by Choe Je-U. The Donghak movement arose as a reaction to Seohak ("Western Learning") and the introduction of Western ideas and Christianity to Korea. Donghak called for a return to the "Way of Heaven" and to traditional Korean ways of living and thinking. In 1892 the small groups of the Donghak movement were united into a single peasant guerrilla army, the Donghak Peasants' Army. The peasants worked in the fields during the day, but at night they armed themselves, raiding government offices and killing rich landlords, traders, and foreigners. They confiscated their victims' properties for redistribution. Their struggle was mainly against foreign invasion and occupation. However, their revolution was put down in 1895 by Japanese forces. Son Byong Hi, who had served as a commander in the Donghak movement, sought political asylum in Japan after the second leader of Donghak, Choe Si-Hyeong, was executed in 1898. Before Choe's death, he had named Son Byong Hi as the third leader of the Donghak movement.

Upon his return to Korea in 1904, after the Russo-Japanese War, Son Byong Hi established the Jinbohoe ("Progressive Society"). Its goal was to reform society and reverse the declining fortunes of the nation. Son Byong Hi also changed the name of the Donghak movement to Chondo Kyo in 1905, in order to display the openness and transparency of the movement and to legitimize it in the eyes of the Japanese. Chondo Kyo was declared a modern religious organization the following year, with its headquarters in Seoul. The primary change that Son Byong Hi brought about through Chondo Kyo was the unprecedented collaboration between Chondo Kyo, Buddhist, and Christian groups in Korea to set up an underground network of rebellion against the Japanese occupation. His efforts culminated in the Sam-Il movement, when the Korean Declaration of Independence was publicly proclaimed at Pagoda Park in Seoul. This ignited a nationwide movement of peaceful demonstration against Japanese oppression. The demonstrations were brutally put down by the Japanese forces, leading to many casualties and arrests. Eui-Am hyeong honors Son Byong Hi's dedication to his country and his efforts in the struggle for Korean independence.

– Yon-Gae (49 movements):

Yon-Gae (Yeon-Gae) hyeong is named after a famous general of the Goguryeo dynasty, Yon-Gae Somoon (603 – 666 C.E.). Yon is a historically controversial figure. The controversies surrounding him revolve around two issues: his character and his role in the fall of Goguryeo. On the one hand, Yon was very successful in defending Goguryeo from the Chinese Tang troops. On the other hand, he staged a coup d'état in 642, killing King Yeongnyu of Goguryeo and placing his nephew, King Bojang (reign: 642 – 668 C.E.), on the throne. Using the new king as a puppet, Yon was the de facto ruler of Goguryeo until his death in 666.

After his death, a struggle for succession between his brother and three sons ensued, which weakened the country. Under General Kim Yoo-Sin, the combined Silla and Tang forces conquered Goguryeo in 668. Traditional Korean histories describe Yon as a despotic leader, whose cruel policies led to the decrease of his population, and whose disobedience to his monarch led to the fall of Goguryeo.

Yon-Gae hyeong honors Yon-Gae Somoon's military achievements in defending his country against the Chinese. The 49 movements of the hyeong refer to 649, the year in which he destroyed nearly 300,000 Tang troops at Ansi Sung, forcing them to retreat to China.

– Moon-Moo (61 movements):

Moon-Moo (Munmu) hyeong is named after the 30th king of the Silla dynasty. Moon-Moo (626 – 681 C.E.) was the nephew of the great General Kim Yoo-Sin, and he ascended the throne shortly after Baekje had been defeated by Silla. The 61 movements in this pattern represent the last two figures of 661, the year Moon-Moo came to the throne.

King Moon-Moo had to face the challenge of freeing his kingdom from Chinese Tang domination. After the Tang had assisted Silla in conquering Baekje, the Tang forces remained in Baekje. The Tang formed the Protectorate General to Pacify the East and attempted to place the entire Korean peninsula, including Silla, under its rule. Many years of struggle against the Chinese followed, and eventually the Silla were able to drive the Chinese out of the Korean peninsula. In 668, Silla was able to unify the parts of the peninsula south of the Taedong River into one kingdom. Moon-Moo reigned over the unified Silla until his death in 681.

On his deathbed, he abdicated in favor of his son, Prince Sinmun. Before he died, he said: "A country should not be without a king at any time. Let the Prince have my crown before he has my coffin. Cremate my remains and scatter the ashes in the sea where the whales live. I will become a dragon and thwart foreign invasion." King Sinmun did as his father asked, and scattered his ashes over Daewangam (the Rock of the Great King), a small rocky islet off the Korean coast.

– So-San (72 movements):

So-San is the pseudonym of the great monk Choi Hyong Ung (1520 – 1604 C.E.) of the Yi dynasty. So-San was a Seon (Zen) master and the author of a number of important religious texts, the most important of which is probably his "Seongaguigam." The "Seongaguigam" is a guide to Seon practice, which is studied by Korean monks even today. The 72 movements of this hyeong refer to So-San's age when he organized a corps of monk soldiers with the assistance of his pupil, Sa Myunh Dang.

At the beginning of the 1590s, Japanese Shogun Toyotomi Hideyoshi made preparations for a large-scale invasion of Joseon (Korea), after Joseon had rejected Japan's request for aid in conquering China. Joseon was unprepared for the approximately 200,000 Japanese soldiers who invaded in 1592, and the Waeran (Japanese War) began. When the invasion started, King Seonjo fled the capital, leaving a weak, poorly trained army to defend the country. In desperation, he called on So-San to organize monks into guerilla units. The presence of So-San's army of monks, operating out of the Heungguksa temple deep in the mountain of Yeongchwisan, was a critical factor in the eventual expulsion of the Japanese invaders in 1593, and then again in 1598.

Timeline of Korean history in relationship to the hyeong:

2333 B.C.E. founding of Korea (old Joseon) by Dan-Gun (according to Samguk Yusa)	Chon-Ji Dan-Gun	
57 B.C.E.– 668 C.E. Three Kingdoms of Korea: Silla, Baekje, Goguryeo	Won-Hyo Hwa-Rang Kwang-Gae Yon-Gae	Ge-Baek Yoo-Sin Ul-Ji Moon-Moo
668 C.E. – 935 C.E. Unified Silla period (corresponding in size closely to present-day Korea), with Silla in the south and Balhae in the north, 698 C.E. – 926 C.E. (including the north of present-day Korea and parts of southern China and Russia). This period is also called the North and South States Period		
918 C.E. – 1392 C.E. Goryeo dynasty	Choi-Yong Po-Eun	
1392 C.E. – 1897 C.E. Joseon dynasty	Yul-Gok Toi-Gye Choong-Moo Choong-Jang Se-Jong So-San	
1897 C.E. – 1910 C.E. Korean Empire	Do-San Joong-Gun	
1910 C.E. – 1945 C.E. Japanese rule over Korea	Eui-Am Sam-Il Ko-Dang	
1919 C.E. – 1948 C.E. Provisional Korean Government in Shanghai		
1945 C.E. – 1948 C.E. Military governments	Tong-Il	
1948 C.E. – present North Korea and South Korea		

Hyeong can be seen not only as an exercise to increase physical ability and focus one's mind, but also as a form of meditation in movement. When the practitioner submerses himself fully into the form, all his mental capacity is directed towards the movement. His mind is occupied with executing all the movements properly, thus leaving very little room for distractions. The inner monologue is quieted, and the concerns and distractions of everyday life disappear.

All movement in Taekwon-Do can be perceived as meditation in movement, but hyeong in particular act as a tool to unburden oneself from the inner chatter and the weight of thoughts by giving the mind a purpose. Initially, the practitioner uses his mental capacity to recall and execute the movements correctly. This leaves no space for distracting thought. Hyeong offer an alternative to the more commonly recognized meditation poses of sitting or lying down. For many people, it is difficult to let go of thoughts while the body is still. Moving one's body offers the advantage of meditation in movement; one is not forced to stop thinking, but rather thought is directed to everything and nothing at once. This state of moving without conscious thought or reasoning is called "mushin" or "no-mind."

Once a hyeong is mastered, the movements no longer require active thought to be executed. Movement happens without conscious command. It is as if the body moves itself, rather than the mind dictating body movement. This helps to attain mushin. This state of no-mind is hard to understand without experiencing it; it is a concept seemingly foreign to the Western mind that cherishes intellect and rational thought. However, achieving this state of mushin, even for a short while, can help alleviate stress and bring about a sense of inner peace and freedom that can last beyond the training session. Eventually, this state should linger longer, ideally permanently, and help one to cope with the stresses of everyday life.

Meditation in movement is not an escape from one's mind. There is no escaping from oneself. Rather, it is akin to a breath of fresh air, a break from the distractions of life. It is a way to bring focus back to oneself after putting oneself out in the world. It can also be seen as a cleansing ritual, both physically and mentally. Through sweating and deep breathing, toxins are carried out of the body. And on a deeper level, hyeong cleanses the practitioner from worries, concerns, and mental ballast.

In everyday life, we are led farther and farther away from the physicality of ourselves and into virtual worlds. Intellectual efforts are valued more than physical efforts, and many jobs require extended hours of sitting. This creates an unhealthy way of living as our bodies are meant to move, adapting to changing impact and changing body postures. Enforced stillness counteracts the fluidity of one's system and leads to rigidity in body, mind, and spirit. Every day, we are presented with limitations of what our bodies are allowed to do. Most jobs do not require the full range of motion, maximum speed, or power possible. Without practice, there is atrophy, imposing limitations on the movements of which human bodies are capable. Hyeong offer a way to bring the practitioner back to himself and confront him with the reality of what is and what is not. The practice of hyeong is a way to break free from the shackles of conformity and offers a vehicle to express the full potential of what human bodies are capable of.

In some hyeong, there are jumps or jumping kicks. Not all jumping kicks practiced in Taekwon-Do are found within hyeong, but the jumps available are a good representation of the various techniques. Most hyeong showcase simple jumping kicks with no more than a 180° rotation; for example, the turning jumping sidekick in hyeong 15 (Ul-Ji hyeong). These jumping kicks are the foundation for other, more spectacular jumps. The higher the skill of the practitioner, the more rotation, height, distance, and force he can add to his jump. This way, opponents can be reached who seem to be out of range. In modern Taekwon-Do, jumps have become increasingly acrobatic to help promote Taekwon-Do at demonstrations. However, these techniques are purely for demonstration purposes and have no application in real life or combat.

Refined jumping kicks are a sign of accomplishment in Taekwon-Do, but they also add a psychological component to Taekwon-Do training. Overcoming gravity, even for a short while, has a great impact on the consciousness of the individual. Living in a world full of limitations, constants that define one's reality, can be oppressive. To overcome gravity with one's own power is a greatly empowering experience, and has the power to change the perspective of the individual. There are a few constants one cannot change in life—for example, eating, sleeping, breathing, and death—but defying gravity for a short while can help to regain a sense of control over one's body, over one's life and destiny. Gravity is one of the greatest influences that shape bodies and minds. To defy it is to defy life, fate, and dependency. Through hyeong, through interpretation of a particular form, the practitioner can experience freedom from limitations, release from containment.

In the display of a form, the consciousness of the practitioner is revealed. The way the movements are executed, the speed, precision, and engagement one shows in the form give precise feedback as to the current physical state and state of mind of the practitioner at that particular time. With changing age and mental development, interpretation and execution of hyeong change as well. With increasing knowledge and practice, individual movements carry more meaning for the practitioner and represent a variety of different interpretations. Many movements can be understood and applied in different ways. Different masters emphasize varying interpretations of particular movements in hyeong to differentiate their own method of teaching and underlying philosophy from other teachers or schools.

The ideal for the practitioner is to learn to express himself in a set pattern of movements and achieve perfection in its execution. Taekwon-Do strives to achieve perfection. The practitioner dedicates himself to its pursuit; however, perfection is never attainable. The process of nearing perfection, getting as close to it as possible, is the appeal. There are similar ideas in Western culture, such as the cave allegory of Plato's "The Republic." There is always room for betterment, improvement of oneself, which requires constant change, constant forward movement, and evolution of one's mind, body, and spirit. To achieve perfection would correspond to the end of evolution, negating the need for practice, and, more so, life itself. This eternal struggle for improvement can be represented by the uroboros, the mythical snake that eats its own tail—as the snake tapers to an end, the head, the new, consumes the old and begins anew; in mythology, the new is not a repetition of the old, but an improvement thereon. Imperfection is within human nature, but at the same time so is the longing for improvement.

The format of hyeong facilitates focus and refinement, not only in one's movements, but also within one's consciousness. Hyeong create unison between body, mind, and spirit. They create harmony between these parts that define human beings. But this harmony, this balance, is a state that differs from one individual to another. When movement is adjusted, the homeostasis of the body is also adjusted, creating a new state of what is and should be considered "normal." The refinement of movement and increased agility, flexibility, and strength refine our state of mind at the same time. Body posture and static individual holding patterns affect consciousness; altering them will change the way one thinks about oneself. The Taekwon-Do practitioner can literally learn how to hold himself differently. Altering body posture affects self-image and emotional states. A simple example is smiling—smiling elevates one's mood, even when one does not feel happy prior to smiling. Through the proper alignment of one's posture and the utilization of a wide range of motion, health is increased and maintained. Since the body functions on a "use it or lose it" principle, it is important to maintain as much of the maximum range of motion as possible. This will not only affect health, but also self-esteem. Memorizing hyeong and executing them with grace can be a great achievement that has a positive impact on one's consciousness. To attain knowledge of hyeong and master the associated technique is not only a feat of memory, but also of controlling one's body. This is one way for a practitioner to take back control of himself. Through hyeong, one adjusts oneself to create harmony in body, mind, and spirit. Harmony is not a fixed state; it is motion. When one adjusts one's body, the state of balance and harmony are adjusted as well. It is a state that differs from one individual to another and it should be recognized that, though similar in each individual, is it not the same for everyone.

2. Taeryon

Sparring in Traditional Taekwon-Do is typically practiced without physical contact. In the traditional conception, sparring requires a foundation of mutual respect and trust that one's partners will not infringe on one's physical integrity. The same applies to competition sparring matches. Today, many dojangs have adopted light-contact point sparring in tournaments. To maintain the traditional respect for practitioners' safety, tournament sparring requires protective gear to prevent serious injury. In Traditional Taekwon-Do, many techniques are deemed to be too dangerous even with light contact. Finger strikes to the eyes are an obvious example, but so are many kicks used in the Traditional style. The points of impact in Traditional Taekwon-Do kicks differ from other styles that have adapted more of a "slap kick" technique; Traditional kicks are designed to cause serious injury when executed properly, which is why it is safer and more practical to practice and perfect these techniques without person-to-person contact. Contact should only be made on conditioning surfaces, such as forging posts, punching bags, and other training equipment.

Sparring is usually introduced to the practitioner when he reaches the rank of green belt, which typically takes about a year of regular practice to achieve. At this rank, he should have enough knowledge of and control over his movements to be capable of practicing no-contact sparring safely. There are three different types of sparring, which differ in the degree of regulation and structure of practice: step sparring, free sparring, and self-defense.

2.1 Step Sparring (Ilbo, Ibo, Sambo Taeryon)

Step sparring is divided into three categories: ilbo taeryon (one-step sparring), ibo taeryon (two-step sparring), and sambo taeryon (three-step sparring). The attacks are always prearranged and the number of steps an attacker moves forward is determined by which category of step sparring is being practiced (ilbo, ibo, or sambo). In response to an attack, usually a single right hand punch towards the head in ilbo taeryon, the opponent must first show a defensive or evasive maneuver and then counterattack with one or more techniques. However, only the initial defensive move should include contact with the attacker. It is a mark of skill for a practitioner to counterattack without touching his opponent. Using this format, technique can be practiced with another person. It is like a dialogue between the two parties as the attacker and defender switch roles after each attack–defense sequence.

For the beginning student, this is a highly controlled format with very limited defense sequences. Different styles of Taekwon-Do, and different dojangs within a style, have their own particular sets of step sparring that they teach as part of their curriculum. Often each belt rank is required to memorize a series of step-sparring defenses which need to be performed at belt-promotion testing. At a later stage in training, with a growing understanding of technique and its variations, the practitioner begins to express his own creativity in technical application. This involves shifting away from choreographed movement patterns to free-form defenses that are suitable for the attacks.

In the dojang I studied in, no standard step sparring was taught. Even though taeryon was required at belt testing, the choice of movement sequences for the defense and counterattack were always left to the individual practitioner. This freedom of choice constitutes an indicator of a practitioner's level of development in Taekwon-Do, and of his state of consciousness. From a practitioner's choice of responses to an attack, an instructor can determine how much of the art the student has absorbed, and which aspects of Taekwon-Do are the most interesting to him. There are four basic defensive responses to an attack: dodging, blocking, simultaneous counterattacking, or re-directing the blow. After the defensive maneuver, one or a set of offensive movements follows. Depending on the personality of the practitioner, his skill level, talents, knowledge, and physical condition, he will lean towards utilizing one type of defense. The same applies to the counterattack after the defense. Thus a practitioner's overall attitude and knowledge of Taekwon-Do are unconsciously displayed through the choice of technique shown.

An attack should focus on the vital or vulnerable spots of the body. Thorough knowledge of these locations separates the student from the master. Counterattacks should be placed accurately and appropriately. The practitioner should display self-control at all times and not show aggression, inappropriate techniques, or uncontrolled behavior. Every movement in Taekwon-Do should be executed with a calm state of mind. A practitioner's posture and facial expression should reflect this. It is important to maintain one's composure and dignity while performing technique. Any emotional turmoil can distract from the movements that are being performed and can lead to accidents and even injury. Because of this, self-control is the most crucial aspect of step sparring. An individual practicing Taekwon-Do should strive to focus only on Do while training in the dojang, leaving all distractions outside.

When judging the quality of step sparring, it helps to ask oneself these questions: How controlled is each movement? How accurate are the movements, and how close to the attacker, without actual contact, are the movements executed? Are spacing and timing correct between attack and defense? Which of the vital spots of the body are attacked? Is the technique used appropriate for a given spot? How fluid is the execution of the sequence of movements? These questions are helpful tools to evaluate the level of skill and understanding the student holds. The higher the level of accuracy, speed, closeness to the partner, and overall flow of movement, the deeper the understanding. When step sparring is performed skillfully, it has great aesthetic value. It shows grace and an accomplishment of physical mastery that is fascinating to watch.

Ilbo taeryon is probably the politest and noblest structure of partner training in Taekwon-Do. The practice of step sparring is a clear representation of the Taekwon-Do philosophy. It shows mutual respect for the understanding and interpretation of Taekwon-Do each practitioner holds. A practitioner's understanding of, interpretation of, and skill in Taekwon-Do is symbolized through their handling of an attack. While the defending partner is executing his technique, the attacking side should not move after the initial attack; this demonstrates trust in the abilities of the other person and gives him a stable target to practice on. It is dangerous for the attacking side to move after the attack is executed. Flinching or other movement after an attack can lead to accidents, as the defending side does not calculate extra movements in his defense; it is expected that the attacker will remain still after the initial attack. However, an advanced practitioner is expected to react and adjust to possible variations; accidents only happen through lack of control and spatial awareness.

Step sparring creates a relationship between two parties. Their techniques are a means of communication, which indicate a level of mutual trust and understanding. Through repetition and working with a steady partner, reactions and skill level become clearly understood, allowing techniques to be executed at a very close distance. This increased understanding of ability increases trust in both step-sparring partners; the attacker becomes less likely to flinch or use defensive gestures while the defender becomes more able to execute techniques at close range without risk of injury. Constant practice eventually allows for closing the distance between the body of the attacker and the limbs of the defender to a fraction of an inch. This requires full focus and attention to each movement. As in all aspects of Taekwon-Do, inattentiveness and/or lack of proper technique can lead to injury; but in this case, there is the risk of injuring another person as well as oneself.

It is important to evaluate skill appropriately and take a step back if one's partner is too close to execute a technique safely. Practicing step sparring requires constant introspection and accurate self-assessment of skill. Over-estimating one's own skill can cause another person harm. Underestimating one's skills can lead to stagnation. In essence, step sparring is a method of perfecting technique, accuracy, fluidity of movement, spatial awareness, self-control, timing, reaction, coordination, spacing, and creativity. But in a much deeper sense, it is symbolic of accomplishing a goal while not infringing on the pursuit of other people's happiness and well-being. Sometimes, taking a step back, leaving a little more space between oneself and another person, makes all the difference. This symbolism is a life lesson that can and should be taken outside of the dojang and applied to everyday life.

Step sparring is also a lesson in how to express oneself, one's ability, and one's knowledge to the fullest extent possible within a given framework while working to maintain self-control. This practice makes step sparring the precursor to free sparring.

2.2 Free Sparring (Chayu Taeryon)

Sparring is one of the primary attractions for most people to begin practicing martial arts. Confrontation with an opponent is not only a practical application of one's knowledge, but also a test of one's skills. Through such confrontations, a practitioner learns to make quick decisions and immediately deal with the consequences of those decisions. The consequences of making the wrong choice in a real-life confrontation can be grave, and can lead to injury or even death. In the safety of a structured environment such as a dojang, this risk is minimized. In modern sparring, it is a matter of winning or losing rather than living or dying. Defeat in a bout carries more emotional than physical trauma.

In Traditional Taekwon-Do, sparring is practiced without contact. This forces a practitioner to acquire control over his movements. Every strike and every kick should stop as close as possible to a sparring partner without actual contact. This emulates striking a target while maintaining the safety of both partners. Other styles of Taekwon-Do incorporate full-contact or semi-contact sparring. Contact sparring has become the focus of many Taekwon-Do schools as they prepare their students for competitions. Contact sparring has its value, but it does not represent the traditional understanding of Taekwon-Do.

Traditional Taekwon-Do's strict adherence to no-contact sparring has raised criticism from other styles of Taekwon-Do and other martial arts. The primary criticism relates to the question whether Traditional Taekwon-Do is effective "on the street" or in full-contact matches. With the rise in popularity of full-contact fighting, more and more people debate the advantages and disadvantages of any particular style. Often, comparisons are drawn between different types of martial arts to determine which is superior. With the rise of social media and the internet, the comparison of the various martial arts, at least superficially, has become very easy. There is a large pool of information available about the different martial arts.

When Taekwon-Do was founded, the only way to learn about Taekwon-Do was to study it in person. Techniques could only be learned through an instructor who decided if a student was ready to learn certain techniques. The same applied to the other martial arts. Now the exchange of information from all parts of the world is virtually instantaneous. Accessing information online can be inspiring and raise the overall level of knowledge of a practitioner, but it can also distract from the importance of finding a dojang and a skilled instructor to properly study Taekwon-Do.

Competition sparring today is very different from Taekwon-Do's nascent years. Now practitioners in the ITF and WTF have global competitions, and the overall number of practitioners is exponentially higher. Taekwon-Do has found its way into full-contact rings and onto movie sets. Its kicking techniques are used in mixed martial arts training and are no longer exclusive to Taekwon-Do. How then can Traditional Taekwon-Do compete with modernization and keep its traditions alive? How effective is it compared to other martial arts or for defense on the street?

The answer is very simple. Traditional Taekwon-Do is very effective once it is understood and the practitioner is well trained in it. Yet one must realize that it takes time and patience to master it. Taekwon-Do presents the practitioner with all the tools necessary to successfully defend himself or stand his ground in the ring or on the street. However, the proper application of a technique needs to be understood by the student so that he can make the necessary mental connections and practice his technique appropriately. Traditional Taekwon-Do requires self-control; it is easier to hit a target than to have enough mastery to stop a kick or a punch just before impact.

It is a sign of the mind undeveloped in Do to seek the "best" style in which to train. There is no single style that would encompass every aspect of and/or be superior to any other style. Truly dedicating oneself to a particular martial art will turn out a great martial artist, regardless of the style in which one trains. Every person has to choose his personal "best" style and commit to it.

Taekwon-Do practitioners should strive to respect the efforts and beliefs of others, and learn from them in order to improve our own art. With modern technology, the opportunity to glimpse the works of other martial arts and learn from them has grown. Taekwon-Do has changed tremendously since its beginning, and it is necessary to appreciate the fact that it is alive and evolving. However, its roots and philosophy should not be forgotten. If the traditions and the way of life of Taekwon-Do are lost, there is only Taekwon. The Do must be kept alive, for without Do, Taekwon becomes mere violence. I believe that the availability of information at our fingertips is a great gift to improve our skills and, at the same time, a great challenge to not stray from what Traditional Taekwon-Do truly is.

One should always remember to look within rather than without for comparison. The strongest opponent one will ever find is oneself. Overcoming an opponent in the ring is only a short moment of glory, but Taekwon-Do is meant to create glorious moments throughout the life of the practitioner. Sparring should be just one of the practices of Taekwon-Do; it is up to the individual dojang or master to decide how much emphasis sparring receives. Many students are not concerned with this aspect of Taekwon-Do; they train for different reasons. However, one of Taekwon-Do's intentions is to permit a practitioner to overcome bigger, stronger opponents. Sparring is the stylized representation of a real conflict between two or more people, and thus a practical application of the teachings of Taekwon-Do.

On the battlefield, a wrong decision in a confrontation will most likely result in the loss of one's life. Yet, in these times, hand-to-hand combat is no longer a decisive factor on the battlefield, as long-range weapons have replaced the need for direct physical interaction with an opponent. Today's battles are won by pressing a button or pulling a trigger, not through face-to-face combat. Because of this, sparring has taken on a much more personal, almost spiritual, aspect. It allows a practitioner to measure his strength and skill against another person. He learns to gauge his level of skill and understanding, and gains the ability to read another person's body language and anticipate his next move. Sparring also includes an element of confidence, and one learns to become more confident with additional sparring practice. To facilitate the safe practice of sparring, Taekwon-Do has set rules in sparring practice and tournaments that allow students to practice and fight with minimal risk of injury.

Much like dancing with a partner, the movements of no-contact sparring need to flow into each other so that there is no clashing of limbs. If sparring is trained in this way, it becomes a battle of wit and skill, rather than one of force. To outwit and outmaneuver another person this way can be compared to playing chess, but using body, mind, and spirit. Sparring is very similar to step sparring in this regard; however, in this case, attack, defense, and counterattack are in constant motion. The four different ways of dealing with an attack remain the same—dodging, blocking, counterattacking, and re-directing the blow—but the number and type of attacks are unknown and unplanned. Every reaction has to be instantaneous; there is no time to think about the next move.

In the beginning, it is difficult for the student to execute his technique correctly and on point. Through practice, he learns to see openings in his opponent's guard, and to recognize and anticipate movement patterns and preferred methods of attacking and defending. If a sparring partner is not skilled in hiding his intentions, an experienced fighter will be able to read his opponent fairly quickly, giving him the advantage. Yet even with this knowledge, timing, speed, and the right choice of technique are the most crucial aspects of sparring.

In sparring, the most vulnerable time is the moment of attack. It is common for a beginning student to focus only on his attack, and forget to maintain his guard while attacking. This leaves him open to a counterattack while he is preparing his own attack. With growing experience, the practitioner will learn to feint or deceive his opponent in order to trigger a reaction that will create an opening in his opponent's guard. This directly translates into all other aspects of life. If one is overly confident in one's approach, one might leave oneself vulnerable to a counterattack. Overconfidence is often the downfall of a practitioner. In sparring, the practitioner learns to harness his confidence and apply it at the right time. Correct timing is the most important aspect of sparring and of life in general.

It is a great exercise to learn how one's own body movements can trigger reactions in others. In addition, extrapolation of this knowledge for application in everyday life can help resolve conflict through words rather than action. Consider the following: If my opinions clash with the opinions of another person and I simply assert that I am correct, it is unlikely that I will be able to convince him of my point of view. In contrast, using the right arguments at the right time and with the right delivery will increase my chances of success. Further, if one approach does not produce the desired result, I should try a different one, instead of repeatedly relying on the same argument. Debate is basically mental sparring, attempting to coax another person to lower their guard—"consider my argument"—for long enough to achieve my goal.

This brings us back to mushin. The mind has to be calm during sparring. Once a practitioner loses control over his emotions, he will become reckless and lose the match. The mind should be as calm as a still lake reflecting the moonlight. The calm lake is a representation of a Taekwon-Do practitioner in the state of mushin, while the moonlight symbolizes the state of his partner. If the practitioner has attained mushin, he will be able to respond to any attack. Any "ripples" in the lake of his mind will distract from mushin. To focus on any thought or emotion during sparring will distract the practitioner and lead to the presentation of an opening for the partner to attack. Here, control over the mind is as important as control over the body. In the state of mushin, movements happen without mental reasoning. Reactions occur first, and the logical explanation of these movements follows later. Body, mind, and spirit are one. This creates a state of being present with oneself to the fullest.

In everyday life, people are bombarded by a multitude of distractions that take them away from their own physical beings. Sparring is one of the most immediate ways back to oneself. Adults and children are constantly tempted to, and sometimes required to, escape into virtual worlds, forgetting about the physicality of their own beings. This is not a healthy state. Through Taekwon-Do, and especially through sparring in Taekwon-Do, practitioners are brought back to themselves. Sparring generates stress in the system that focuses on the individual. As one is faced with a real attack, a real threat, concentration returns back "home" into one's body and mind. There is no faster way to turn off the extraneous chatter of inner monologue than the threat of being punched or kicked in the head.

Once centered within himself, a practitioner learns to deal with one of the most primal emotions: fear. The fear of being physically hurt is ever present in all practitioners. The secret is not to avoid fear, but to manage it, to use this fear to avoid becoming reckless. The more sparring one engages in, the less prominent fear becomes. Lack of fear during a confrontation leads to the overestimation of one's skill, losing the match, and / or injury. Yet overcoming one's initial fear of sparring builds great self-esteem and courage. In real-life applications, sparring teaches a student to stand up for himself, to stand his ground in necessary confrontations, and to have the confidence to walk away from unnecessary confrontations.

It also helps him to realize the inherent connection between himself and his sparring partner. Once another person is acknowledged as another human being, once a connection is established, it is difficult to willingly harm that person. In sparring, two partners create a unit. They create a whole and are a representation of the movement of yin-yang. During sparring, a similar balance between fear and confidence occurs internally. The tension between fear and confidence shifts within the individual as he changes back and forth between attack and defense, creating an overall state of equilibrium. Sometimes one is more pronounced than the other, but the fluctuation between the two is requisite for the practitioner to be successful.

The same principle applies to striking and kicking. Every blow dealt should be moderated and controlled. Every blow received should illustrate the impact one's techniques have on another person. This leads to learning to value and respect the physical integrity of another human being and should facilitate the practitioner becoming a more peaceful person. Experiencing the effects of one's actions on other people and on oneself leads to the realization that all of one's decisions can have potentially helpful or harmful effects. The ability to make decisions in real life will be enhanced and accelerated by this knowledge. In sparring, there is no time to thoroughly think through a response; the practitioner is forced to come to an immediate decision and then deal with the consequences of that decision. He needs to quickly learn to assess his own skill level and the options of appropriate responses with the tools available to him. If his guard is lowered or a move is made, the sparring partner will give prompt feedback to any opening in his defenses with an attack or counterattack. Sparring, especially with a stronger, more experienced opponent, teaches a practitioner to quickly assess himself and his abilities. In everyday life one is faced with many decisions. Occasionally a particular decision is feared because of its possible consequences. However, the advanced Taekwon-Do practitioner should not be indecisive, neither in sparring, nor in life. If he is well centered in himself, an answer will quickly arise; the fear of potential consequences that arises will help guide us to be cautious and attentive.

Sparring is always trained at the dojang and under supervision. This ensures that sparring is conducted in a safe and controlled environment. The beginning student will lack self-control and require an instructor's experience to guide sparring practice to prevent physical contact. Also, sparring should always be practiced with mutual respect and awareness of the sparring partner; an instructor should insist on the observance of proper protocol. If students are too casual or inattentive during sparring practice, the risk of injury increases dramatically.

Students who are caught fighting outside of structured Taekwon-Do classes or events—other than for the purpose of legitimately defending themselves or someone in need—should be demoted in rank and, in severe cases, expelled from the dojang. Taekwon-Do does not encourage the desire to fight others. Conflict is a necessary part of life, but it should be handled calmly and with appropriate measures. Seeking conflict will lead to finding it and, eventually, to suffering from it. Sparring in Taekwon-Do is meant to improve an individual in body, mind, and spirit, not to suppress another person for personal gain. When fighting an opponent, winning should not be the main focus of the practitioner, as it will distract him. In battle, there was no winning or losing, only survival. Focusing on winning will lead away from mushin. It is like a Zen koan: The practitioner will win, though he does not think about winning, and there is nothing that can be won. When the practitioner has attained mushin, winning or losing will not matter. He will simply be, and his body will respond. Wanting to overpower another person will not help him to win a competition, as he will lose mushin through his intentions. In Taekwon-Do, one's power should never be used to put another person down or to force one's will upon somebody else, but to better oneself. All the physical, mental, and spiritual strength that one achieves through Taekwon-Do should be used to enhance and protect life.

2.3 Self-Defense (Ho Sin Sool)

Self-defense, much like sparring, is another main attraction for people to start studying Taekwon-Do. It constitutes the practical application of this art and reduces it to its most simplistic state. In its beginning stages, Taekwon-Do was used mainly for military training; many of the pioneers of Taekwon-Do had ties to the Korean government. It proved to be a very effective system of hand-to-hand combat against armed and unarmed attackers. In modern self-defense, function is the main focus of movement, rather than art. It reduces Taekwon-Do to its most primal state, where effectiveness is the only standard of measurement.

The philosophy behind self-defense in Taekwon-Do relies on the Ippon System—one punch, one kill. It focuses on how quickly an opponent can be disabled through minimum effort. A single strike or kick should be powerful enough to achieve this, which requires thorough training and conditioning of the hands and feet. In self-defense, the focus is to produce maximum effect through minimum effort.

Taekwon-Do teaches a practitioner to disable one or multiple opponents who might be bigger or stronger than he is. Even though there is no weapons training in Traditional Taekwon-Do, defense against armed attackers is taught to prepare the student for the possibility of an emergency. Hosinsul is a mini-malistic approach to dealing with an attack. In learning, practicing, and teach-ing self-defense techniques, the following questions can be used to assess the effectiveness of each technique: Does it work for everyone? Does it work all the time? Does it work under all circumstances? If the answer to each question is yes, the technique is truly effective.

With increasing knowledge of Taekwon-Do, the practitioner gains a wider spectrum of techniques available to choose from to handle different situations. The technical array that the individual practitioner has at his dis posal will become more refined and intricate. Also, his arsenal of responses to any given attack will grow. However, there are only a limited number of vital spots on the human body, and only a few of them are available for attacking at any given moment. Through extensive training, the student will not only learn to recognize these, but also to strike them accurately and with appropriate force. If one understands the body and its functions properly, it is fairly easy to find the right spots on another person to attack and disable them quickly.

Often, when self-defense is demonstrated, practitioners display tech-niques that are very appealing and entertaining to watch, but not very effective. The fastest and easiest ways of disabling or injuring another person are not pleasant to watch and are not usually demonstrated because of their brutality. Taekwon-Do incorporates these techniques into hyeong and during everyday technical training, but they are not always obvious as such to the beginning student. An advanced practitioner understands the underlying self-defense applications of hyeong. If one takes the art aspect out of Taekwon-Do and reduces it to martial technique only, then it becomes a very powerful tool for defending oneself.

The moral and ethical education of the Taekwon-Do student is very important, so he learns to restrain himself from using excessive force during a defensive situation. Any response to an attack should be immediate and forceful, but appropriate. In a real-life self-defense situation, there are no second chances. Speed, accuracy, and the element of surprise are the strongest weapons available.

Training for a real defensive situation can be stressful for the individual, even if it is conducted in a controlled setting. However, being put under stress allows the practitioner to learn to remain calm during a real confrontation. In the dojang it is possible to create scenarios that simulate real-life attacks without risk of injury. This helps the student to feel ready and prepared, and raises his confidence and self-esteem. This feeling of preparedness boosts the confidence of the practitioner; it gives him the feeling of being in control of his own life and not dependent on the arbitrariness of others.

Through training, practitioners learn to manage the fear that arises in a confrontation. Fear is essential, and assists with making the right choices. However, fear should not rule one's mind or cloud one's judgment. One does not practice Taekwon-Do in order to live in a state of alertness, to be prepared to thwart hostile attacks at any given moment. Instead, a student learns to be aware of his surroundings, avoid conflicts before they arise, and defend himself only when necessary.

As mentioned above, it is important not to use excessive force and not to continue fighting after an attacker has been disabled. An attacker should only be harmed to the extent necessary to stop the attack. This restraint shows respect and compassion for human life, even toward people who intend harm. One should only injure, disable, or even take the life of another person if there are no other alternatives.

In the old student passports—booklets that recorded rank promotion, events attended, and tournament accomplishments, as well as the system rules and dojang policies—that were given out by the Kwon Jae Hwa Taekwon-Do association, one of the student rules was: "never kill unjustly." This refers back to the code of the Hwa-Rang, the "Knights of Korea." Taekwon-Do does not argue that it is morally or ethically right or wrong to take the life of another person, but asserts that killing is justified only if the situation warrants it. This creates a grey area, as there are many factors to be considered when determining whether a situation justifies killing another human being. The Taekwon-Do philosophy clearly states that another person should only be killed when there is a serious threat to one's own life or to another person's. However, taking a life should be the last option; disabling an attacker should be the first priority. This is the real-life application of the core principle of Taekwon-Do.

Taekwon-Do is a defensive martial art, which is not to be used offensively. This is symbolized often in hyeong, step sparring, and instructor-led combinations, as many Taekwon-Do practices begin with a defensive technique. Further, most self-defense situations can be avoided entirely, making physical confrontation unnecessary. Taekwon-Do teaches the student awareness of himself and his surroundings so potential threats can be identified and avoided. Through politeness and humility, many conflicts can be deflated before they escalate.

One of the most important aspects of self-defense is self-confidence. Once a state of inner calm and confidence is achieved, one does not project the image of either a victim or a threat to others. Threatening situations are likely to become scarce, if not cease altogether. The overall manner in which a practitioner carries himself changes the interaction between his space of existence and the concepts and opinions he holds about it. Low self-esteem leads to conflict in life. Conversely, to treat oneself with dignity and compassion is to treat one's entire space of existence with dignity and compassion.

Sometimes it requires more courage to walk away from a confrontation than to become involved in it. The Taekwon-Do student learns to keep his composure and dignity and walk away from confrontations over trivial matters. This reflects the strength of character and respect for others learned in the dojang. Confidence and healthy self-esteem are important aspects of self-defense that can obviate the need for good technique. If one does not see oneself as a victim, one will not project this image to others, and will then be less likely to be victimized. One should always remember that the best sword is the one that never needs to be drawn.

3. Breaking (Kyek Pa)

For the observer, the breaking of material is one of the most spectacular displays of Taekwon-Do. It is a trademark of Taekwon-Do, as well as other East Asian martial arts, to break a variety of materials with different body parts. Breaking is an integral part of most Taekwon-Do schools, as different breaks are required for belt testing. Each belt rank has specific breaking requirements, which increase in difficulty of technique and skill as rank increases. Breaking is also performed during various occasions aside from testing, such as demonstrations and tournaments. Even though it would appear that breaking is a significant part of Taekwon-Do, it is rarely practiced during regular training.

Breaking should never be done for the purpose of feeding one's ego; there is a much deeper meaning to it than just smashing material. Ostensibly, the primary reason for breaking is to test the Taekwon-Do practitioner's ability to apply his technique correctly. Since no contact is allowed in training or sparring, breaking constitutes a measuring tool for the effectiveness of the student's techniques. It allows for the full strength of a technique to be applied on material without the risk of injuring another person. With progressing belt ranks, students are asked to demonstrate breaking with more demanding techniques. This ensures that their technique is not only correct, so students do not hurt themselves during its execution, but also that the technique has enough force behind it to inflict substantial damage on another person. The types of breaks required to progress from each belt rank to the next vary depending on the school or the organization one is affiliated with. For example, in my school the first board-breaking technique required of the student is the side kick (yop chagi).

Different breaking materials are used to demonstrate different techniques and amounts of force, but the most common material is wood.

Students in Germany break pine boards of 1" thickness each for women, and 1.5" for men. In the U.S., all boards are 1" thick, due to the lack of availability of 1.5" wooden planks. With increasing progress, the Taekwon-Do practitioner can test his skill on multiple layers of boards, or select harder materials such as concrete, brick, or river rock. Usually, after a student has reached black belt, he chooses the techniques and the types and amounts of material for demonstrating breaks.

In order to break harder or more material, the practitioner needs to condition his "tools" first. The points of impact on the hands and feet need to be strengthened and callused to minimize the risk of injury. Before the practitioner can perform a successful break, he needs to prepare himself for it. This includes preparing the body through conditioning on a dallyon as well as practicing technique. This also means that he needs to prepare his mind and spirit. Only if all three parts align can a break be completed successfully. It requires patience and dedication to build up the necessary prerequisites for breaking. It is fascinating to watch a master breaking a river rock, but the truly impressive aspect about this is the years of training and the dedication to Taekwon-Do that make such a feat possible.

Initially, the master decides when a student is ready to perform a certain break. As the student progresses and eventually starts teaching himself, or opens his own dojang, he needs to be able to gauge his own level of skill appropriately and choose breaking techniques and materials accordingly. Overestimating one's skill or underestimating the density or hardness of material can lead to injuries, like broken hands and feet. Taekwon-Do is meant to build up and maintain health, so it is crucial to prepare the body and not to attempt breaks prematurely. Many students are initially reluctant to put in the work necessary to be properly prepared to execute certain breaks, so it is up to the master to remind them of the importance of conditioning and technique training. The student has to be guided to a state where he can make choices for himself without endangering his health and well-being. Inevitably, though, he will have to bear the consequences of his choices. The right technique and the right material are crucial decisions for breaking without injury. Only through guidance by a knowledgeable teacher and his own experience will a practitioner have the ability to make the right decisions.

Breaking is, at its core, an exercise in alignment of body, mind, and spirit to overcome matter with skill and personal responsibility. It is also an expression of the individual's mastery of technique; breaking should demonstrate the ability of the practitioner to overcome matter with technique, not with brute force. Breaking material becomes a self-imposed challenge of the mind. It is a battle against one of the most primal fears: the fear of pain. When breaking, the mind needs to be empty of all passions and distractions. The complete focus is on technique. In the mind, the material should be broken before any movement begins. There is no room for any doubt or hesitation, as these will lead to failure. This state of absolute focus, of emptiness and fullness at the same time, has been described as "satori" in Zen Buddhism. This concept has no equivalent in Western cultures and to describe it succinctly is complicated. However, an approximate translation of "satori" is "enlightenment." It is the state of realizing the true nature of being and self. Satori is the first step toward reaching salvation and access to Nirvana. The state of mushin that Taekwon-Do training facilitates for the individual is a prerequisite to experiencing satori. Taekwon-Do strives to achieve a state of satori within the practitioner. In breaking, it is expressed by performing a single action and achieving this state in a single moment. All mental, physical, and spiritual force is concentrated and focused on one single spot. In breaking, we concentrate our entire being into one movement.

No bone in the human body is strong enough to break a rock. Only through the alignment of technique, speed, precision, and focus on a small part of the body at the time and point of impact can the breaking of dense material be achieved. This accomplishment also requires all the energy generated from the Ha Bog Bu, and the state of mushin. At the point of impact, the yell "Kiap" increases the release of the accumulated physical, mental, and spiritual energy during the execution of the technique. Matter can be overcome through technique, even if it seems impossible.

Often one hears stories of people achieving extraordinary feats that might not be considered possible by normal standards. These all have one thing in common: the state of being that the person was in at that moment. In extreme situations, we are capable of reaching our maximum potential. If in need, we are able to generate more strength, speed, and dexterity than normal. Taekwon-Do training allows the practitioner to reach this potential more frequently and, at the stage of a master, makes it constantly available. With time, practice, and mastery, breaking becomes a spiritual exercise that pushes the boundaries of what might be physically possible, not through brute force, but through refinement of technique and the attainment of satori.

III. Training Taekwon-Do

There are three primary physical facets of Taekwon-Do training: technique, stretching, and conditioning. These aspects incorporate everything that can be done with and to the body to achieve greater skill, stamina, power, agility, and speed. As such, they form the core of training. And through physical training, the process of change also occurs in both mind and spirit. It is the conditioning of the soul, the process of becoming one with oneself, that allows the individual to encompass his entire being and create harmony within himself.

1. Technique

Taekwon-Do training as an intellectual exercise is a complex notion. Most Taekwon-Do training is conducted non-verbally; instruction most often involves observation and the repetition of exercises. Traditionally, very little explanation of technique, let alone philosophy or spirituality, is given during classes. And students should not ask questions as they might be disruptive to the flow of the class. However, there is no substitute for proper physical instruction in the dojang with a qualified instructor. Taekwon-Do philosophy and pedagogy need to be understood through its practice. This puts the responsibility of extracting these concepts from training on the student. The irony in this is that at certain belt ranks, the practitioner is expected to know that which is never explained.

In Traditional Taekwon-Do, there is no formal instructor training or philosophy "class." No recommended reading list is available, and philosophical guidance tends to come only in the form of scoldings given to students. In Traditional Taekwon-Do, all training involves physical application. Very rarely is there an opportunity for the Taekwon-Do philosophy to be discussed. The student is expected to simply know, but how can one achieve greater understanding if it is not taught? The only way for a student to understand the Taekwon-Do philosophy is to look at and extract from the example his teacher is setting. This introduces an element of the instructor's personality into the student's interpretation of the Taekwon-Do philosophy. It is sometimes difficult to distinguish between these, making a true understanding of the Taekwon-Do philosophy even more complex.

Contrary to tradition, I believe that there needs to be personal, intellectual discussion and reflection on the training experienced. Students need to understand what they are learning, not only follow instructions blindly. Teachers should be open to explaining aspects of Taekwon-Do when students have difficulties understanding them. Class is not always the appropriate time or place to have these discussions; however, instructors can make time after class or while stretching to go over the concepts underlying the techniques of Taekwon-Do. Meanwhile, students should maintain a curious mind and seek to develop themselves at all times. This includes an understanding of what and why they are practicing, as well as improving their technique. In and around training, students hear different statements about the Taekwon-Do philosophy; it is their responsibility to make the connections among those pieces of information.

One of the catch phrases that Taekwon-Do often promotes itself with is that training will close the gap between body, mind, and spirit. Yet this process is never explained. Furthermore, I disagree with the idea that there is a gap. There is no schism. These three aspects of a human being are inseparable. The student should not begin training with the feeling of lacking something. There is no lack of harmony or balance, there is just a need to become more aware of oneself and to return to a more natural state of being. Children are in this state already and, over time, learn to suppress and forget about this state of being. One needs to remember what one is at one's core, and to experience the joy and pleasure of the physicality of one's being.

Moving one's body should be a pleasurable experience. Even if training is hard and physically challenging, every student should enjoy the experience. Through training, people learn to experience the pleasure of moving their bodies at maximum speed, range, and force possible on any given day. Daily life limits each person to a fraction of what they are physically capable of. Attending training sessions helps people break out of the physical, mental, and spiritual limitations of their day-to-day routines.

Taekwon-Do is meant to empower people through training. Students learn to adjust their current state of being to a more contributing state in which they increase the possibilities of their abilities. Taekwon-Do training adds to their range of motion, speed, power, flexibility, and technique, but each healthy person already has all the necessary requisites available within them. It is just a matter of learning how to use body, mind, and spirit to reach one's full potential. At its most basic, Taekwon-Do training is a way to learn to utilize one's body in a different fashion.

Students begin by learning basic techniques and, initially, it is simply that: technique. Students learn how to stand, walk, fall, and move their limbs and their entire body in a different way than before. The beginning student will perceive learned movements as something separate from him until he has incorporated the techniques to a certain degree, at which point they become part of his regular movement repertoire.

At first, he learns individual movements and, later, strings of movements that allow him to expand his capability of movement. Students begin training with the capabilities required for daily life. Through Taekwon-Do training, students acquire an entirely different set of tools to work with. Each basic singular technique can be perceived as a new tool. A punch, for example, would be a new tool. Through various movement experiences, students learn how to apply their bodies and their entire system—body, breath, mind, and spirit to certain patterns and situations by using these new tools.

Later, an understanding of technique grows and movements are connected to meaning rather than mere mimicry and repetition. This adds a symbolic layer to the use of acquired tools, which creates a mental bond between movement, meaning, and memory. Once the student attaches a piece of intellectual information, an emotion, and the sensory memory of execution of movement to one specific technique, it becomes truly internalized. A movement will have multiple qualities that trigger certain internal reactions and emotions within the practitioner. Eventually, performing a certain movement or movement sequence will trigger specific mental and emotional states in the individual. In this way, one is able to influence mood and consciousness through movement.

Finally, the label "technique" dissolves in the consciousness of the practitioner, and is replaced by an acknowledgment that a movement is just a movement as it occurs. Once technique is fully adapted internally, it becomes part of one's natural way of moving. This is when the individual encompasses the "techne" portion of technique; this is the point when movement becomes an expression of art.

First, the student learns technique.
Then, the student knows technique.
At the end, there is no technique. Technique is nothing and everything at the same time.

The difference between student and master in terms of Taekwon-Do technique is not evaluated by the amount of muscle power or flexibility. It is movement experience and the heightened capability of using one's body that identifies a master. Muscle mass and flexibility can easily be increased; however, those are not the important criteria of what constitutes great movement. The amount of coordination and control that a master has acquired through training makes his movements superior to those of a student. Additionally, the degree and understanding of mental and spiritual integration that a master has achieved is illustrated through observation of his movements. Reaching this state requires time and effort; however, once internally integrated, it remains with the practitioner for life.

In periods of non-training, physical power, flexibility, and speed are the first to atrophy. Since the body functions on a "use-it-or-lose-it" principle, a practitioner needs to maintain the status quo within his body through a minimum of training; otherwise, his muscle mass and flexibility will decrease. However, these can be quickly regained once training is reinitiated. Muscle memory, coordination, and control will remain with the practitioner to a certain degree, even during extended periods of inactivity. He might forget the right sequences of movements in the hyeong, but the basic ability and understanding to execute them remains. To change the physical status quo, the impact of training needs to be increased.

Taekwon-Do training shapes our bodies on the surface, but on a deeper level, it shapes our consciousness. Since all techniques and movements are linked to a purpose and a meaning, training is not mere body movement.

All parts of the body are engaged. This is what constitutes the difference between Taekwon-Do training and lifting weights, jogging, or playing sports. Taekwon-Do is a holistic way of working with the body.

The range of movements and muscle groups utilized during Taekwon-Do training is much greater than in any other form of exercise. Control of the body plays a large role in Taekwon-Do: Improving coordination, balance, and gross motor skills, as well as fine motor skills, are integral parts of Taekwon-Do training. Through this training, students learn to control their limbs and entire body to perform many actions that seemed difficult, or even impossible, previously. Having control over his body gives the practitioner a feeling of control over his own life. It enhances his self-esteem through the simple fact that he can impact his own existence.

In daily life, there is little room for personal expression, let alone control over the events that surround and impact an individual. True personal freedom would come at the price of being excluded from society. Through control over his own self, a Taekwon-Do practitioner regains some of that freedom by controlling his space of existence and his being. The ability to consciously move one's body allows for the experience of personal freedom. Leaping kicks play a large psychological role in such expression. They are a symbol of defying the ties that bind a student to this existence. For a short period of time, he can escape the inevitable constants of his life using his own strength and through control of his body.

Through exercise, one feels an increase in overall well-being. The endorphin and adrenalin rush that is generated through training increases happiness and the ability to cope with frustrations. Beyond the hormonal benefits of training, there are many physiological effects that occur within the body that increase the overall health and functioning of the body. Taekwon-Do training increases circulation, appetite, digestion, and detoxification, and balances out mood swings. Psychologically, students feel empowered through the ability to use their bodies to their maximum potential, which results in an increase in health and happiness. Movement becomes conscious and spontaneous, rather than compulsive.

Moshe Feldenkrais, who dedicated his life to studying movement and its effects on the health of the human body and psyche, examined movement and posture and developed his own method, the Feldenkrais Method, to work with the body. His method tries to facilitate change within the body through conscious movement, and analyzes individual movement components. It is a subtle and gentle method that attempts to positively affect the physical and psychological conditions of the individual. Feldenkrais was one of the pioneers of Judo in Europe, and examined its movement applications and benefits for his work.

If understood well, Taekwon-Do can achieve similar effects. Taekwon-Do is a way of working with the body and achieving change for the individual. Since martial skill in itself is no longer the primary focus of Taekwon-Do, a paradigm shift can engender the perspective of Taekwon-Do as a different type of bodywork, a new way to restructure movement and understanding of the body, mind, and spirit in order to increase the overall health and well-being of a practitioner.

Once movement reaches a certain stage of refinement, students are able to eliminate all unwanted movement patterns from their system. This also affects unconscious body language, giving the individual more control over how he communicates with others. The famous mime Samy Molcho researched body language extensively, and provides a comprehensive reference for how body posture and language impact mood and interactions with others. A key finding of his research is the importance of awareness of one's movements and what these movements communicate to others.

The body is a manifestation of consciousness. Once one alters the state of one's body, one alters one's consciousness. The feeling of control a student experiences through the ability to make conscious movement choices directly translates into a feeling of being in control of his life. One can only manage one's own space of existence. Most maladaptive mental challenges that people face stem from a feeling of powerlessness in life. Feelings of dependency and depression that many people experience can be alleviated through Taekwon-Do training. Once capable of controlling one's own inner universe, it becomes easier to navigate the outside world. An inner sense of control and feelings of heightened self-confidence and self-efficacy lead to an ability to respond to external frustrations in a healthy manner. If an individual does not believe in himself, it becomes more difficult for him to stand his ground in the outside world and deal with daily life. By contrast, if one does believe in oneself, interactions with other people improve and navigation of life's complexities becomes more manageable. If a practitioner has a strong sense of self-value and is happy about his own state of being, his manner of dealing with people will improve. Further, if he values his own well-being, he will understand the value of others' well-being and will be more likely to strive to maintain healthy relationships.

This has multiple implications for self-defense. Firstly, if a practitioner has high self-esteem, he will project this to others through his body posture and demeanor. Thus, he will be less likely to be victimized by others; if he appears strong and confident, others will be less likely to attempt to harass or assault him. Secondly, if he has high self-esteem, he will be less likely to fall prey to peer pressure that may lead to dangerous situations. And thirdly, if he has a strong sense of self-worth, the law of attraction indicates that he will try to surround himself with similarly positive people. Therefore, the likelihood that he will be exposed to possibly threatening situations decreases.

For the spectator, most Traditional Taekwon-Do classes appear to stress technique training, rather than working on heavy bags or doing strength-building exercises. Sparring is not stressed during most practice sessions, though sparring- specific classes are occasionally offered. What the spectator is unable to see are the internal processes that happen within the student during each class.

Classes that are complicated in terms of technique are intended to train the mind rather than the body. Simple punch-kick sequences can be learned quickly by a beginner as these require little thought. Once he has mastered the basics, he begins to learn more intricate movement patterns. Training becomes a mental challenge in acquiring, internalizing, and executing movement sequences accurately and quickly. All sequences are created using the basic movements and techniques of Taekwon-Do. And though the individual segments of combinations have already been mastered by the practitioner, the mental challenge is to quickly recombine what he already knows into something new. The less active thought a practitioner needs to process a new combination, the more quickly and accurately he can repeat it. Once a high level of integration of individual Taekwon-Do movements is achieved, recombining them into new sequences should be effortless and instantaneous. This constitutes the master level of Taekwon-Do.

At the black-belt level, new combinations of techniques should be grasped and repeated immediately, without the need for practice. This includes learning new hyeong as well as training combinations. However, this does not mean that the practitioner does not need to practice a new technique after it is learned. On the contrary, the practitioner should constantly try to refine his technique. This includes studying the composition of each combination, the mechanics of its technique, and its effects on the body. Every combination consists of a particular sequence of movements and the activation of several muscle groups. It is helpful for the student to practice only parts of particular movements to facilitate their proper execution. For example, if one of the core muscle groups for a combination is inhibited and the practitioner cannot achieve full extension of an arm or leg in a certain position, it makes sense to focus on that particular segment of the movement in order to train the muscle group until the student can reach full extension. This focused training involves subtle movements and requires increased awareness of the body. It also requires time that an instructor often lacks during classes. Depending on class size, the time an instructor has for attending to individual students is fairly limited. For this reason, self-training becomes a vital part of Taekwon-Do.

In essence, all Taekwon-Do training is self-training, with the addition of guidance at the dojang. The more a student practices on his own, the faster he will progress. At a dojang, the student receives corrections from his instructor and then is able to work on refining his technique independently. The dedication and discipline to self-train is crucial for the advanced practitioner, especially as one moves into an instructor role. Most of the training that an instructor receives is of his own making. Even though it is a challenge to continue training in addition to teaching classes, it is necessary in order to maintain a certain level of training as instructors continue to be students of the art. Refinement never ends, and a Taekwon-Do teacher should have the willpower and dedication to train for himself. Continuing training is a hallmark of a true master.

Traditional Taekwon-Do is considered a "hard style" in comparison to other styles of martial arts such as Kung Fu or Tai Chi. Most movements involve a wide range of extension, flexion, and/or rotation. The end of each strike, kick, or block contains a snapping motion to introduce torque and increase power. For a beginning student, it is difficult to relax his muscles during the execution of a movement and only tense up immediately prior to the point of impact. Continued training makes this easier, and it eventually becomes a natural part of one's movement patterns.

Even though Taekwon-Do might appear to be hard on the surface, the practitioner should be in a relaxed state most of the time. Without the proper release of the antagonistic muscles, a movement is hindered or inaccurately performed. Learning to relax certain muscle groups to allow movements at high speeds is a very important aspect of training. Physically, this involves training only sequences of movements, or single movements, to achieve optimal agonist-antagonist muscle coordination. Mentally, this requires letting go of resistance patterns that might lead to muscle tightness in certain areas of the body.

This is another representation of the yin-yang principle. A practitioner has to find softness in hard movement, he has to learn to let go while maintaining control of his movement. The right balance of soft and hard is necessary for fast and strong movements. One cannot exist without the other, and without both sides being in harmony, movement will be a struggle. To facilitate understanding of this for the student, the teacher should have knowledge of the body and its functions. Very few instructors have a background in anatomy, physiology, sport sciences, or biomechanics. I believe that to be able to teach Taekwon-Do properly, an instructor should acquire at least a basic knowledge of these areas. If official study of these is not feasible, an instructor should analyze the movements he teaches and become aware of their effects on the body and the human psyche. Realizing how a certain movement makes one feel and which muscles might be sore after training is a good starting point. In this way, training can be adjusted to avoid non-contributing movements or exercises which might lead to injury.

Technique in Taekwon-Do has many layers of meaning and application, from physical strengthening to mental strengthening to spiritual growth. In later stages of training, students have to transcend technique. Technique should move the student, rather than the student directing technique. Once technique starts moving the student, he can move with presence and awareness. His mind should not resist this motion. He should not stop mentally or physically to analyze that which is moving him. This is meditation in movement. As the mind is occupied with feeling the movement, there is no room for other thought. With this, students reach a state of fullness rather than emptiness; they are aware of all that they are without consciously thinking about it. The fullness of being completely oneself consists of total awareness of breath, heartbeat, blood flow, the spinal pulse, movement of the organs, and even movement of individual hairs on the body; all thoughts, emotions, memories, everything that is in the space of existence receives awareness, yet there is no specific focus on any one of them. Such a state consists of a feeling of fullness of and connection with everything that one is, while being simultaneously empty and detached. This is mushin.

It is not easy to stop the inner monologue, to reach emptiness of the mind. Rather than attempting to consciously let go of the chatter, Taekwon-Do directs all focus into individual movements. By placing the mind in the movement of the moment, the chatter is naturally quieted: By giving the mind a job, it is kept occupied and therefore distracted from the stresses of daily life.

It is not possible to fully suppress one's emotions and thoughts, but through attaining awareness of and control over his body, a practitioner can choose when and to what extent to engage in them; he can choose the time and amount of energy to dedicate to them. One should not be taken over and ruled by one's emotions. While neglecting them completely is unhealthy, one should control them and learn to express thoughts and emotions in the appropriate time and manner.

2. Stretching

Stretching means stretching the entire being, not just stretching the muscles. The physical body is a focal point for the manifestation of mind and spirit at a given point in time. This creates a combination of everything that a person is in the moment, and everything that he was and everything that he will become.

If one understands this concept, stretching will shift many things, physically, mentally, and spiritually. The expansion one reaches through stretching the muscles and increasing the range of motion expands one's perception and increases one's range of existence, as well.

Individual concepts, perceptions, and judgments about life and reality impact the physical being; conversely, the physical being impacts concepts, perceptions, and judgments. Hence, old or non-contributing concepts can change through modification of the patterns of posture and movement. Changing the range of motion influences change in one's perspective, leading to a change in existence.

Through the beliefs and concepts a student maintains, he develops certain ways of holding himself. This leads to various effects on body, mind, and spirit. It can increase physical capabilities, but also lead to ill health or injury if one's concepts become too rigid. At birth, the human body is extremely flexible. It is pliable and open to new experiences. The mind is the same. Growing up, one has many different movement experiences that will make up the foundation of all of one's understanding of movements. One's genes, the circumstances of one's childhood, one's particular life choices, and the demands of society will lead to certain holding and moving patterns. These factors can enhance flexibility in body, mind, and spirit, or they can lead to certain postural deficiencies and muscle hyper tension. The combination of an individual's experiences, beliefs, and circumstances strongly influences the quality of his mental, spiritual, and physical health.

The body is designed to resist the constant pressure of gravity, which means that any postural changes made in one part of the body will inevitably lead to a readjustment of the entire system. The sub-cortex's sensors responsible for static alignment are constantly trying to maintain its "normal" posture through a minimum of effort. Depending on the individual, that posture varies. What would be considered normal posture is a very individualized state. The body constantly tries to maintain homeostasis. However, certain postures will lead to certain effects on the rest of the body, especially the internal organs. Posture can be optimized, just as movement can be.

In Taekwon-Do, reorganizing a student's posture is not a static exercise; it consists of a combination of factors, including learning proper technique and fluidity of motion, and engaging in a variety of exercises. Repetitive movements and exercises both physically and mentally create rigidity in thoughts and beliefs. This manifests directly as rigidity of the body. Further, one-sided postural impact on the body will have a non-contributing effect on a person's well-being. This is why Taekwon-Do trains both sides of the body equally. Since most of the body's mass is composed of water, it is important to maintain a status that matches the fluidity inherent in the body. Fluidity in the body translates to fluidity in the mind. Taekwon-Do should consist of both changing impact on the body and stretching, to avoid rigidity and one-sidedness.

Looking at the complexity of what constitutes a human being, several layers emerge: the physical body, the psychological body, and the spiritual body. Taekwon-Do works primarily with the physical body, and tries to reach the conscious, subconscious, and spirit through physical training. Psychological training or counseling is not a focus of Taekwon-Do. The Taekwon-Do instructor is not meant to interfere in the private life of his students. However, working with the body can be seen as a "back-door" approach to altering the psyche of a practitioner.

Psychological aspects of an individual's Taekwon-Do training can be addressed through his studies, but never directly. Stretching is a very gentle, yet effective way to affect the emotional and psychological state of being in an oblique manner as changing the body changes the way one thinks about one's existence. Some of the things people carry inside them might be too painful or scary to look at directly. Through stretching, the practitioner will not only experience increased flexibility, but also psychological release and reduced tension. An example is the correlation between neck or back tension and one's mood. An overly tight neck will leave the individual feeling "choked" by his own muscle tension. This tightness will not only impair blood circulation to the head and lead to a decreased ability to think, but will also lead to headaches and a poor emotional state. The feeling of being choked will depress the mood and decrease openness to interaction with others and willingness to learn. Once tension in the neck is released, normal blood flow resumes, the headache dissipates, and the mood of the individual is elevated. Relaxing the body will relax the mind at the same time.

Attaining a greater range of motion can lead to greater confidence and self-esteem. If one is in tune with the way one's own body responds to all aspects of one's life, subtle changes can be achieved very quickly through simple adjustments of posture. Increasing the range of motion is one of the key aims of Taekwon-Do, and it can increase the range of motion in other aspects of one's life. In this regard, Taekwon-Do is very similar to other types of bodywork that facilitate change, both physically and mentally. Rather than passive adjustment of the body by a skilled practitioner as in massage, chiropractic work, acupuncture, or bodywork, in Taekwon-Do, the individual is responsible for achieving change through active movement. He cannot hand over the responsibility to engender change within him to an outside source; he is responsible for achieving it himself. Stretching is an essential activity to accomplish this. Yet stretching remains an underestimated and underappreciated part of Taekwon-Do training.

Flexibility of all parts of the body is necessary to improve certain aspects of training. For example, fast turns require flexibility of the back, shoulders, and the neck. Relaxation of the muscles around the hip and the pelvis is crucial to achieving more efficient footwork and higher kicks. While building strength and dexterity in the muscles increases speed and power of movement, flexibility and relaxation increase the efficient use of these muscle groups. Stretching refines movement to achieve greater efficiency with less effort. In order for a muscle to be able to fully contract, hence developing its full potential, its counterpart must be able to fully relax. A perfect counterbalance has to be achieved so one muscle group can move freely, without the resistance of its opposite. If a muscle group does not want to comply with what is required at a particular moment, or is even resistant due to an inability to retract, a less than optimal result will occur. In many cases, this leads to injury.

Even if the affected muscle groups have not had a chance to properly warm up, they will cooperate during a movement, provided that an individual is balanced and has a relaxed muscle tone. Nevertheless, one should be wary of abusing one's body, and not try to force muscle groups into action without a proper warm-up. This might lead to bruising or even tearing of the muscles. In a fight against yourself, you always lose.

The basic principle of stretching is to hold each stretch for only a short while, or to give short stretch impulses, when warming up to assist with contraction of the muscle for increased performance. At the end of class, each stretch pose should be held for a longer period of time—one to two minutes—to cool down and to give the muscles a chance to relax. Additionally, one should focus on using breath properly while stretching to assist with the relaxation of the muscles. Holding one's breath tightens targeted areas, which counteracts the purpose of stretching. One should melt into the stretch, allowing the body to adjust itself to the sensation rather than forcing the body into a pose. With each exhalation, it is helpful to visualize exhaling through the points of tension in the body. This focused breathing lessens resistance to the stretch and also keeps the mind occupied and focused during stretching.

Venturing into an increased range of motion of a particular muscle group can cause memories and emotions to be released. One might encounter a wide range of emotions, including joy, fear, anger, hate, love, elation, sadness, and even grief. Old and new memories that have been stored in certain physical spaces might surface. It is good to allow these memories to arise, but not to hold on to them. Working with the flow of the breath, one can gently dissipate the memories and emotions during exhalation.

Holding a stretch for a long time can put a practitioner in touch with his thoughts, memories, and emotions in amazing and unexpected ways. The muscular release experienced through stretching releases the tension holding on to these mental and emotional aspects. Staying in a stretch for an extended period of time is a way of staying within oneself. However, one should not force one's body into positions or actions that it is not prepared for; there will be a price to pay for that later on.

The intensity of each physical experience is individualized, and it is important not to attach labels to what is being experienced so that one can be wholly immersed in each sensation as it is occurring. For example, labeling a body sensation as "pain" is a very unspecific, unhelpful term. Pain is a socially constructed word that describes a variety of body sensations that we have been taught to label as pain and that consists of a variety of different sensations and intensities. For everyday use, the term pain is essential to describe discomfort, but lacks specificity as it encompasses many different qualities.

It is important to evaluate the quality of a sensation closely; to taste it, smell it, see it, touch it, hear it, and feel it, to fully immerse oneself in the feeling and allow it to be. It is healthy to accept what is inside of one's body and to expand and refine it, not to break or conquer it. Once one understands the multitude of sensations that are pain, one will not fear them as much. This gives the individual more control over himself when in a state of distress as he can more clearly identify what is happening to him. This is another layer of knowing oneself and one's different states of being.

Stretching is one of the most important and yet most misunderstood aspects of martial arts training because the benefits are not fully comprehended by most practitioners. It tends to be seen only as a way of extending one's physical range of motion; it is not understood as a tool for mental, emotional, and spiritual growth. In comparison to Yoga practice, which has a deep philosophy behind it, stretching in Taekwon-Do is merely treated as a necessity to reach a specific goal; it is work that needs to be done to get where one wants to be physically. Yet stretching is a way to increase awareness of oneself, get to know who one is, and acknowledge oneself holistically.

Stretching exercises are more similar to Yoga than is commonly recognized. Through stretching, a student can discover areas of the body that are tight and explore their connections to other muscle groups. For example, tight hamstrings can lead to back pain as they attach to the sacrum and the pelvis. Releasing the hamstrings will not only increase the height of a front kick, but can also release the lower back. Due to the interconnectedness of the body and its internal structures, tightness can occur in areas that seem unrelated to certain movements. It is important to handle these areas gently and stretch with compassion. This includes having compassion for oneself, respecting temporal limitations, and taking the time to explore one's own body. Ideally, the whole body should be addressed when stretching, which should occur regularly. If a full body set is not possible every day, one should set a few minutes aside each day for selected stretches specific to sore areas.

Taekwon-Do does not focus on stretching as much as other practices, such as Yoga, but it is a fixed part of the daily training routine. Usually, only basic stretches are taught during the warm-up. As there is not enough time during a class to cover every aspect of training, teaching technique takes priority over stretching. To counterbalance this deficit and improve overall flexibility and well-being, the practitioner should try to stretch his entire body at least once a week. Stretching has many positive physical effects such as increased agonist–antagonist muscle coordination, detoxification, increased muscle recovery, and injury prevention. Most importantly, it is a way of increasing awareness of oneself and acknowledging one's own body. It is important to take the time to get to know oneself in order to progress in training and in life. Stretching is a way of being with oneself that is accessible to every individual.

3. Conditioning

Mastery of the physical aspects of Taekwon-Do requires a student to prepare his body properly. All aspects of Taekwon-Do are interwoven with each other, and one is not easily separated from another. Conditioning the body teaches the student to persevere, to be steadfast, and to reach a calm state of mind in moments of turmoil. Like sparring and breaking, conditioning is a great tool to raise a student's self-esteem. The old Latin proverb "Mens sana in corpore sano" (A sound mind in a healthy body) applies here. Conditioning can be considered in two ways: the purely physical aspect of conditioning, and the mental and spiritual effects conditioning has on the individual.

There are several methods to train for physical conditioning. The most common is the training of the body to generate more speed, power, and agility. Improvement of these areas is at the core of training for many different types of activities, sports, and other martial arts. The basic concepts do not vary much, but in Taekwon-Do, most exercises are tailored to the specific demands of the practitioner. In training, it is important for an instructor to choose the right exercises to match the current training curriculum, which should reflect the current stage of development of the students. It is also important to introduce new movements; the constant use of similar exercises, which causes stress in muscle groups due to repetition, leads to the overuse of structures within the body such as joints, ligaments, and cartilage that are vital for movement. Variation in practice is necessary.

A well-grounded understanding of the body and its functions should be standard among instructors to assist with knowledgeable curriculum construction. As practitioners are constantly changing in life, so should training. Abilities change with age, and this should be understood and supported in class. Things that are emphasized for the young body might not be suitable for the body of a middle-aged or older person.

The focus of training should not be how much can be achieved, or how well the practitioner is doing, but rather how long he can practice this art. Once 1st Dan is achieved, the study of Taekwon-Do should become a life-long pursuit; commitment to training is a hallmark of the master. Only through the right training methods can this goal be accomplished. The true challenge for a Taekwon-Do practitioner is to reach a high standard of physical achievement, and then to maintain it over the course of years, even decades. The practice of Taekwon-Do is intended to build and maintain health. The non-contact philosophy of Traditional Taekwon-Do is intended to allow the individual to practice for as long as his general health permits. Additionally, Traditional Taekwon-Do takes an inclusive approach toward practitioners; as its philosophy includes improvement of oneself without competition, and provides for increase in skill and rank at the individual practitioner's pace, there are few limitations as to who can train.

Conditioning in Taekwon-Do consists of different aspects. Strength, stamina, agility, speed, and coordination are all routine training goals. Each dojang has its own training routines in place for students, focusing on its specific style of Taekwon-Do. In addition to conventional training methods, such as those that might be found in most sports, Taekwon-Do incorporates breathing techniques and conditioning of the hands and feet. This conditioning is meant to prepare striking surfaces, which include any target area that the practitioner might strike with, for impact. This type of conditioning is most commonly done with a dallyon. For example, the first two knuckles of the fore-fist are conditioned for contact while executing a punch. Repeatedly punching a dallyon generates more callus around the knuckles. It also increases the density and thickness of affected parts of the bones in response to the constant stimulus. It is easy to spot a dedicated Taekwon-Do practitioner by looking at his hands. These "Taekwon-Do hands" are a symbol for committed Taekwon-Do training.

In a Traditional dojang, all training is conducted on hardwood flooring to naturally condition the feet. This is essential for the safe execution of foot techniques. It is not uncommon to find a Taekwon-Do practitioner or master conditioning his hands and feet on a wall or a tree. A student usually starts his conditioning by hitting softer surfaces, like paddles, shields, punching bags, or sand, and later moves on to doing push-ups on the first two knuckles before he starts conditioning on harder surfaces. Conditioning the hands and feet is essential for two reasons: It increases the ability to strike a target with more accuracy and force, and it protects bodily impact points when hitting a target. There are many target areas on the hand and elbow that are used in Taekwon-Do, and it is necessary to condition them all. The same applies to the legs and feet.

Traditionally, only the right hand and foot would be conditioned out of respect for one's ancestors. The left side represents yin, the female element and also the genetic line; the right side represents yang, the male element. Since Korean and most East Asian cultures were traditionally patriarchies, the right side was dominant. Additionally, it was deemed inappropriate to train the left side due to the concept of ancestor worship. Training the left side could be interpreted as disrespectful of one's familial line. Today, however, most practitioners condition both hands and both feet, as conditioning both sides creates a more balanced use of the body. Also, with the increase of popularity of Taekwon-Do in the Western world, many of the cultural values have been adapted to a modern interpretation of Taekwon-Do.

Injuries during breaking happen for only two reasons: lack of skill and/or lack of conditioning. In addition to conditioning the parts of the body used for attacks, the forearms and lower legs, which are mostly used for blocking, are conditioned as well. Again, this can be achieved by striking a dallyon, or with a partner as a coordination and conditioning exercise. A strong blocking technique can break a bone in an attacker's arm or leg and render him unable to attack again. Good conditioning also offers more protection from impact, whether it is during a strike, a fall, or an attack with an object. Taekwon-Do conditioning attempts to prepare the practitioner for impact on both the dealing and receiving ends of a blow. Other parts of the body are conditioned for receiving impact, as well. For example, building up the muscles around the abdomen protects the internal organs from impact. The entire body should be readied to strike with maximum accuracy, speed, and force, and to absorb similar impact, at any given moment, and it should have enough stamina to last until the conflict is resolved or evaded. The Taekwon-Do practitioner should also be physically and mentally prepared to remove himself from danger whenever possible.

Challenging physical training is a representation of the Taekwon-Do spirit to master oneself. However, it is of the utmost importance to not only train hard physically in order to build a strong and healthy body, but also to be mindful of the vehicle that one is using to achieve this. The importance of self-care is often underestimated. Mindful living, the reduction of non-contributing influences, and proper nutrition and rest are necessary to achieve greatness in Taekwon-Do. With exposure to so many temptations in daily life, maintaining a healthy lifestyle poses a challenge for most people. The mental strength to resist temptation is a crucial step in mastering oneself. To ensure the longevity and functioning of a healthy body, one must treat it as a sacred vessel. One should strive to support one's physical, mental, and spiritual training progress with everything that goes inside the body and everything that surrounds it. This is applicable to all matters of daily life, whether it is food, clothing, living arrangements, or the company kept. In order to achieve the extraordinary, we must leave the ordinary behind.

Sometimes one is limited by the availability of foodstuffs and the circumstances of living situations. In these instances, one has to make use of resources to the best of one's ability. To train Taekwon-Do is to live Taekwon-Do, and the lifestyle of the practitioner should continuously reflect his dedication to Do.

4. Mental Conditioning

Not all conditioning in Taekwon-Do is physical. Many exercises have profound intrinsic effects on an individual. Similar to other Taekwon-Do training, conditioning attempts to create mushin in the practitioner. Every movement in

Taekwon-Do can be perceived to be meditation in movement. Also, conditioning strives to increase the practitioner's Ki, or life force. In training, the practitioner is often put in stressful situations, physically and psychologically. Sometimes, a student will be physically pushed to the limit of what his body is capable of, and then expected to go further. This creates dissonance in the mind and body, accompanied by internal warning signals. Pushing beyond these limitations—when the mind has given up complaining about the lack of air, the soreness of muscles, or any other physical distractions—achieves a state of clarity where the mind is no longer interfering with movement. This is "no-mind," or mushin.

Through extreme conditioning, this state can be achieved, even if only for a short while. This accomplishment rewards the practitioner with greater self-esteem, as he is able to overcome his perceived limitations and reach a new state of being. His ability to perform new technique, at greater speeds, and with greater skill confirms this new self-perception, which is accompanied by feeling the sudden ease and lightness of resistance-free movement. Along with other aspects of Taekwon-Do, this moment of breakthrough gives the practitioner additional strength to cope with life. Being aware of what he is capable of, what he can achieve through his own efforts, makes him more settled within himself. Feeling secure internally resolves many conflicts in interactions before they even arise. As a practitioner grows in confidence and his spirit grows stronger, less of what he encounters in life will be threatening to him.

Traditionally, the conquering of limitations was achieved through training methods that involved difficult terrain or harsh environments, such as training in snow or under waterfalls, mountain climbing, or conditioning on trees in the forest. Overcoming these conditions created not only memories and a strong mental foundation for a practitioner, but also the feeling of being able to surmount incredible obstacles in his life. Things that seemed impossible before become possible.

Through conditioning, the body of a practitioner becomes tougher and his tolerance for and acceptance of pain increases. Conditioning also teaches a student to receive a blow without resisting it. Relaxing into a kick or strike attack, letting the impact pass through the body, is a more effective defense and results in less damage than resisting the impact. Resistance creates tension, and tight structures in the area of impact can be damaged; allowing the force of impact to flow through and out of one's body prevents injury. This translates well into real life. Consider replacing a punch with a verbal insult, and consider the ways the recipient can respond to that insult. Muscle or mental tension in response to a verbal attack causes stress and physical discomfort. This can lead to patterns that will have long-term effects on the body and mind. Relaxing into a physical or verbal attack generates a healthier way of being.

In learning to manage the physical discomforts of conditioning, a student learns to compartmentalize physical sensations from his psychological state. Over time, muscle tension or injuries cause less emotional discomfort, and in cases of distress, mental calm will prevail. Once accustomed to and experienced with differentiating "pain" sensations that arise in the body, their impact on one's consciousness lessens. This is mental conditioning.

The greatest fear is the fear of the unknown. Once one comprehends the bodily sensations that have caused prior distress, one can manage them calmly and with compassion. This is the same principle that underlies other aspects of Taekwon-Do. Conditioning is yet another tool to attain control over the body, mind, and spirit. Once a practitioner gains the ability to control all aspects of self, he will also feel that he is in control of his life. Conditioning gives accurate and immediate feedback to the physicality of his being; it brings a student's focus back to himself. A practitioner hardens his body to be ready for physical confrontation, but, at the same time, this prepares him to accept frustration, criticism, and anger from other people. It is conditioning of the soul.

In the dojang, a teacher prepares a student physically, as well as mentally, to grow stronger. Seldom will a student hear praise from his teacher. This lack of external approval teaches a student to not become dependent on others' opinions, and to build self-esteem through his own efforts. A student should learn to accept what praise is given to him with gratitude and humility, and should strive to perfect his skill for his own development. In the course of his practice, a student faces a great deal of frustration and anger. Failure is part of training. Examples include failing to break a board, losing a sparring match, or not mastering a technique quickly. Other times, a student might feel he should be promoted to the next rank, though his teacher does not test him or acknowledge his progress. All the annoyances that training can bring teach a student patience. Practice in the dojang prepares a student to deal with the frustrations of life and to bear them without losing his temper.

Moving the body, working out, and sweating releases pent-up energy, both physically and emotionally. It also allows an individual to find an outlet for his frustrations in a structured environment. Mental conditioning of the student happens in everyday practice, even if he is not aware of it. He learns to discipline his body, and thereby learns to discipline his consciousness. Visually, a master is perceived punching a post or a wall, but on a deeper level, he is forging his body, his mind, and his soul. Conditioning is like forging a samurai sword. It is a cycle of heat, pounding into shape, and cooling off. It involves fire, water, and pressure. If the hammer strokes are too hard, the steel will shatter. If they are too soft, they cannot shape the steel. It takes a combination of determination, sweat, practice, experience, and a lot of patience to make a well-balanced sword.

IV. Teaching

At a certain stage in the development of many Taekwon-Do practitioners, usually after reaching 1st Dan, they desire to teach Taekwon-Do. The black belt not only symbolizes "master," but also "teacher." Achieving black belt reflects a practitioner's dedication and skill, but along with master rank comes the responsibility for the student to pass the art on to the next generation. Giving back by teaching represents one's appreciation for having learned so much oneself. In keeping with Confucian values, a student should first learn to govern himself before governing others. In reaching black belt, he should have sufficient knowledge and ability to do both of these.

Not many students venture on to open their own dojang. It is a major step in life and requires a lot of dedication and commitment as dojang owners must balance teaching Taekwon-Do with running a business. Each student has to decide for himself how passionate he is about the art and how far he wants to become involved in teaching. It is more common for black belts to assist their masters by teaching at an established dojang, or to substitute teach during a master's absence. This kind of assistance is a way of paying respect to the teacher and the school. Traditionally, only one instructor was responsible for all the classes taught at a dojang. Today, many dojangs have multiple instructors who assist the master with teaching.

It is part of one's Taekwon-Do education to learn to teach others. Teaching offers a practitioner a whole new insight into the art. It gives him the opportunity to learn the same thing from different angles, and challenges him to present his knowledge of technique in different ways to make Taekwon-Do accessible to others. This way, a Taekwon-Do student gains a different level of understanding of technique and application. Only through teaching can the student understand certain intangible aspects of Taekwon-Do. Before he starts teaching, a practitioner knows Taekwon-Do only from a student's perspective. He has become proficient in his technique and has developed his understanding of Do to a certain degree. However, technical mastery does not equate to the skill of teaching. Through teaching, a Taekwon-Do student comes to realize how much he still has to learn and how much he needs to progress in order to become a great teacher. The teaching of Taekwon-Do should teach an individual compassion, patience, and humility. He will realize that no matter how great his physical skill and refinement of technique is, he will not be able to assist others in reaching the same if he lacks true understanding of Taekwon and Do. Body and mind have to work at the same time; teaching demands complete focus and attention. A teacher needs to be aware of each student, and to ensure that students' movements are executed correctly. Teaching Taekwon-Do requires different explanations for different students; reaching each student requires depth of knowledge, skill, and creativity. It is the flexibility to adapt to students' needs, the ability to teach technique in various ways, that promotes greater awareness and depth of understanding of a teacher's previously mastered techniques.

Learning Taekwon-Do and participating in classes is a privilege. For some practitioners, it is not until they start teaching that they truly appreciate this. When taking a class, all movement executed belongs to the practitioner himself. Its only purpose is to increase his skill. He can "turn off" his mind and immerse himself in the technique. When teaching, this is not possible. All movements that are demonstrated by the teacher need to be 100% accurate to show the best possible technique, and he must constantly be mindful of the students, the curriculum, and the environment on the training floor. All movements are meant to inspire the students and to set a good example for proper execution. The technique now belongs to the students and the art, not only to the practitioner himself. He has become a representation of Taekwon-Do, thereby losing his personal identity. To indicate this shift in identity and role, beginning at 1st Dan practitioners are referred to by their title rather than their name. This is both a sign of respect and an acknowledgment that personal identity is now less important than a practitioner's commitment to the art and his position in the dojang.

Once a practitioner makes the commitment to teach Taekwon-Do, his only focus should be the progress of his students; how quickly and efficiently he can facilitate an increase in their skill and understanding of Do through his teachings. As an instructor, personal skill only matters in order to demonstrate technique to his students. The instructor needs to surrender himself and his skill to assisting others in their progress. He has to put his personal ego and biases aside, focusing only on the progress of his students. Ostensibly, that means showing technique targeted to the composition of each class. Everything that is shown needs to be appropriate for the students present. The beginning student will not be able to imitate or even understand most of the advanced movements or combinations that the teacher knows. Every class needs to cater to those present; the technique taught should challenge and inspire everyone, without excluding any of the students present. The teacher has to resist his own instinct to move too quickly or to overload the students with his knowledge. Every Taekwon-Do instructor should consider himself a representative of Taekwon-Do and welcome the responsibility that comes with this honored position.

Instructors' behavior needs to be in accordance with the idea of Do at all times. Correct behavior is crucial to teaching Taekwon-Do. Teaching Taekwon-Do involves much more than just teaching technique; it centers on the forging of consciousness. The young student has no framework of reference for what he is learning. Taekwon-Do provides a new set of rules, a new structure, and a whole new paradigm of values. The student is presented with a new code of conduct in the dojang and, in addition to learning to follow these rules, has to learn his place within the hierarchy of the student body. Often there is no handbook to explain the nuances of etiquette. Rather, this learning takes place through modeled behavior. Therefore, instructors, as well as higher-ranking students, must continuously model appropriate behavior and etiquette.

Taekwon-Do is a way of life, and it is an enormous responsibility to teach it. New students experience themselves and their bodies through new patterns of movement, which have an impact on their perceptions of themselves and their reality. It is of the utmost importance to conduct oneself as a teacher in a way that provides students with proper direction in their pursuit of this new understanding of themselves. A teacher has to lead, in word and deed, in a way that presents students with examples to draw upon. Through experiencing a particular teacher's interpretation of this art, students gain access to Taekwon-Do. Over time and with experience, each student comes to a deeper understanding of Do, from which individualized conceptions of Do emerge.

Every style, every teacher, has a personalized interpretation of the Do of Taekwon, and every teacher has to remember the privilege of and responsibility involved in teaching others. He teaches them not just movement and technique, but how to perceive Taekwon-Do. He shapes their bodies, minds, and spirits through Taekwon-Do. Because of the significant impact one instructor can have on a multitude of students, the teaching of Taekwon-Do is a serious endeavor; any behavior or attitude that a teacher displays may be adopted by his students. When new to training, a student's ability for critical thinking and understanding of Taekwon-Do is not developed to the stage where he can differentiate between Taekwon-Do philosophy and the teacher's personality; the beginning student has no basis for comparison. With continued exposure to one master, philosophy and personality can become inextricably entwined in a student's perception of Taekwon-Do, potentially misrepresenting the philosophical underpinnings of the art. This places the burden of responsibility on the teacher to separate his individual personality from the teachings of Do.

Every human being has his own concepts, values, and views on life. An instructor's perspectives might undergo change throughout the course of his Taekwon-Do training, but it is important to be aware of one's conceptual and physical biases. A teacher's private opinions or judgments about students' lives and the choices they make are solely his own, and should be maintained as such. Every verbal judgment made, every opinion voiced about a student, represents a limitation of the instructor's consciousness and carries weight with those who hear these statements. It is wise, necessary even, to choose judgmental statements carefully, even if they appear to be of a positive nature.

Every word uttered in front of students impacts them and has the potential to affect their perceptions of themselves and the art. Young children, especially, learn not only through imitation of movement, but also through imitation of words spoken in their presence. It is crucial to be mindful of one's speech and to choose words carefully. Students who grow up training Taekwon-Do have a tendency to base their perception of the art, and possibly life as a whole, on their master's statements and attitude. This makes sense as the respect afforded a martial arts master should be unquestioned, which extrapolates to unquestioned acceptance of his actions and statements.

Compartmentalization is one of the most important aspects for a teacher to understand and enact. At times, it is difficult to differentiate between one's personal life and Taekwon-Do life, but instructors must strive to keep the different aspects of their lives as separate as possible. For example, it is inappropriate to seek the company of students outside of the dojang for any reason other than Taekwon-Do-related business and events. Casual fraternization with students outside of the dojang can dispel the power differential between teacher and student, potentially complicating the student-teacher relationship inside the dojang. A student cannot be expected to differentiate between seeing and responding to an instructor as his master inside the dojang, and seeing him as a private person outside of the dojang.

The responsibility for distinguishing between private person and Taekwon-Do master lies with the instructor. As he holds the power, he also carries the weight of modeling appropriate behavior. This includes being wary of any boundaries that he might cross. The temptation to extend a relationship with a student to one of informality outside of the dojang can be great. Many students are incredible people, and the desire to get to know them better is natural. However, this can create a dissonance that is a disservice to students and their progress. Few people are capable of truly compartmentalizing the various aspects of their lives, and putting the responsibility on a student to "switch on" when inside and "switch off" when outside of the school is unfair to the student. The instructor needs to create and foster a clear separation between student and teacher. Without this distinction, students unwittingly lose respect for an instructor as master, are likely to carry the casual relationship into the school, and model this poor behavior for other students. A misstep on the slippery slope of caring for one's students that leads to becoming involved in their personal lives can quickly undermine a teacher's position in the eyes of their student body, making teaching more difficult and giving rise to concerns of favoritism.

Regarding favoritism, a teacher cannot regularly devote private attention to specific students while excluding others without upsetting the atmosphere of the school. This includes accepting personal favors from students. For example, if a student offers a teacher a discount at their place of employment, it would be inappropriate for the teacher to take advantage of it unless the purchase directly benefitted the school. All students should be treated equally in their opportunities to learn Taekwon-Do, and any favor accepted from a student should be used to promote the school or Taekwon-Do. Teaching and learning Taekwon-Do requires separation between personal affairs and the dojang; all personal matters should remain outside. A practice at many schools is to remove one's shoes at the door as symbolic of relieving oneself of the day's issues before entering the training space. Paralleling the students' separation of daily routine and Taekwon-Do, a teacher needs to be professional while compassionate, polite, and respectful, without being overly friendly. Each individual student's progress, the continuance of the school and the art, should be the sole focus of the master. Teaching Taekwon-Do can be a lonely path at times, even though a teacher is surrounded by many people every day.

Students are not a teacher's peers. It can be a challenge to maintain an adequate distance from students with whom a teacher works on a daily basis. This is especially difficult with long-term students. It is very rewarding to see students grow up in Taekwon-Do and mark their progress. In the traditional understanding, the student–teacher relationship is a lifetime commitment. Even if student and teacher should part ways, they still retain the relationship of student and teacher. After spending many years studying under a teacher, students become like family to an instructor. It is very difficult to navigate these relationships while retaining an objective viewpoint; the teacher should be cautious as to how involved he becomes in a student's life. For the same reasons, he should also be cautious of giving advice pertaining to matters other than Taekwon-Do, even if the student asks him for it.

It is the duty of the teacher to strive to refine the art that he is teaching and learn from the challenges that students present him with. No teacher should ever consider himself without flaw or fail, as hubris inevitably leads to downfall. One learns through realizing what it is that one does not know. In this regard, a student can be considered a mirror to a teacher's deficiencies. In many instances, an instructor's shortcomings are reflected back at him through the behavior of his students. Often, a teacher initially recognizes flaws in a student, only to realize that he is struggling with the same issues himself. Students are great teaching tools for the instructor, helping him to recognize his own issues, and thus allowing him to better himself.

Teaching requires constant refinement, and mastery of skill does not reflect mastery of teaching; it is an ongoing process. In achieving black belt, a student is humbled as he comes to understand the lack of what he truly knows. In this sense, Taekwon-Do is very Socratic. A master is superior to a student simply because the master has deeper knowledge of what it is that he himself still needs to learn.

Once a student stops refining what he is or what he does, he stops progressing. It is not an accepted aspect of the art to stop one's evolution, as this is contrary to nature. It is important to understand bodies as well as consciousness as dynamic states of constant change and renewal. Water becomes stale when there is no motion in it, and the same applies to the human body. Body posture is a good example of this principle: The body constantly tries to adapt to its state of existence, to find a way of maintaining equilibrium with the least amount of effort. The same concept is applied to movement, and all other aspects of life, when a practitioner allows this natural equilibrium to surface.

In Taekwon-Do training, a student receives instruction from his teacher to improve his Taekwon-Do. Yet the master needs to look at himself at the same time. It is easy to become too comfortable with oneself, finding and residing in the "sweet spot" that permits adequate teaching without conscious effort. It becomes important to engage in self-reflection and self-training. Though it is not easy to find the time or energy to train in addition to teaching every day, an instructor needs to create time for self-improvement, and to seek out further instruction from his master. There is no doubt that teaching progresses an individual's skill and understanding of the art tremendously. At the same time, it is crucial for him to continue to feel the physical effects of training and to reaffirm for himself why he is so passionate about Taekwon-Do. After a student opens his own dojang, taking classes from his teacher becomes a luxury, and he should strive to attend these classes from time to time in order to further his own education. Along with personal improvement and reaffirmation, this brings him the benefit of studying different teaching methods; he can then incorporate this added information into his own teaching, as appropriate. Attending seminars and classes benefits an instructor both as a student and as a teacher; it holistically addresses personal and professional development.

Teaching is a skill that needs flexibility and creativity to cater to different learning styles. Not every student reacts the same way to the same teaching methods. A teacher needs to be flexible in his teaching and adapt his teachings to his specific students. Every teacher is different, and each student should find a teacher who suits him. Every student who walks through the door of a dojang poses a challenge for the teacher; it takes patience and great skill to bring out a student's potential. There are no bad students, only teachers who cannot find the right approach to teach them. Not every student is right for every teacher, or vice-versa. The bond between student and teacher is sacred and it should be treasured, but this requires mutual trust and the willingness to teach / learn. A student who has no desire to learn Taekwon-Do cannot be reached, no matter the skill of or methods employed by the teacher. No progress will come from instruction that is received during involuntary attendance. It is the student's responsibility to be respectful and follow directions to the best of his ability. As much as the teacher has to surrender himself to providing the best possible instruction, the student has to surrender himself to his best possible learning. The more a student immerses himself in his studies, the more quickly he progresses.

One of the greatest sources of potential frustrations for a teacher is to see his students fail to progress as quickly as they could because they are lazy or unwilling to learn. Every student brings a different skill set with him, every student has different talents, but to witness students neglecting their talents is difficult for a dedicated teacher to accept. However, any good teacher will know to separate himself and his personal agenda from his student, and he will not take a student's lack of interest personally. At the same time, the great teacher will find a way to motivate these students.

All students are not equal. As humans, there are tremendous differences between individuals. Many factors such as gender, age, education, and physical skill level make us different. Every student should receive the same level of training and the same opportunities; however, different students learn at different rates, and it is not wise to hold the more talented student back because his peers cannot keep up with his progress. Taekwon-Do instructors should only look at people as people and not through a filter of any sort. Every student should be allowed to study as long as he obeys the rules of the dojang and behaves respectfully. Students should be treated the same, but not equally rewarded. Taekwon-Do holds a meritocratic philosophy: The more effort expended and the more progress a student makes, the more rank he should be awarded.

This meritocratic system includes his attitude as well as his skill level. Students should be judged based on their level of skill, effort, attitude, and maturity. The Taekwon-Do philosophy involves tolerance, respect, and humility. In the pursuit of Do, all people are the same. The only difference is each student's level of achievement. No matter what rank an individual holds, even a master rank, he still remains a student in Do. This is one of the core aspects of the Do of Taekwon-Do. Training never ceases; everybody remains a student of the Do. This should never be forgotten.

In Taekwon-Do, as in life, it is important to focus on what needs to be accomplished at any given moment. For example, newer students are often concerned with achievements and rank, but masters should be able to see their own limitations and strive to transcend them. Every Taekwon-Do practitioner should refine the ability to compartmentalize his training at the dojang. It is perhaps one of the hardest lessons to learn, to separate one's private life from the dojang. Once the student is deeply involved in his training, the dojang will play a very important part in his life. It is hard to separate all the experiences had, all the obstacles overcome, and all the progress made in the dojang from one's private life. Naturally, friendships evolve in the dojang from training together. Training with fellow students at a dojang for a long period of time creates a special bond. All the blood, sweat, and tears shed together create a sense of family in the dojang. This helps students to progress, as they feel a sense of belonging and take pride in their dojang. Without this sense of belonging, students would not be as motivated to pursue Taekwon-Do. People have an inherent need for belongingness, and it is important to teach a sense of community to students. Students should honor their dojang and stay loyal to it.

Traditionally, students would help maintain the dojang at which they were training. This taught the student humility, respect for his dojang, and a deeper connection to the school. Modern methods do not follow this model, so it is important for instructors to find ways to involve students in the growth and care of the school. In this way, the dojang becomes more than a training hall; it becomes sacred space where transformation occurs. This also teaches a student to take responsibility for his own space. In a wider sense, this extends to a sense of involvement in the community in which the student is living. Further extrapolation teaches students that the same sense of belonging applies on a macro scale. We all belong to this planet, we are all people, and thus we should show care for all people. There can be no intolerance of others. The safety of knowing that he belongs fortifies a student's character, so he can share this sense of safety and respect with others. Occasionally, there is rivalry or dislike between students. Yet, they still belong to the same dojang, and thus should show a sense of caring toward each other. Through a negative relationship, students are taught that even their rivals deserve respect; the lesson becomes that of accepting differences and expressing tolerance for diversity.

Teaching Taekwon-Do, teaching of any sort, is a rewarding yet challenging endeavor. This art is only understood through its practice; knowledge without application is incomplete. Further, mere application without reflection results in skill without control, which is one short step away from violence. Mind and consciousness have to be developed alongside physical skill, even though grasping certain ideas is difficult. Much of the philosophy is discovered solely through individual reflection as most instruction is non-verbal. Great skill without self-awareness, self-reflection, or consideration of consequences cannot be deemed mastery.

In traditional training, a student is not allowed to ask questions about what is being taught. My personal Taekwon-Do philosophy diverts from tradition in this aspect. Students should be given the opportunity to ask philosophical questions to facilitate their understanding of Taekwon-Do. While disrupting class to ask these questions is not appropriate, I encourage students to approach me before or after classes. A crucial aspect of teaching is to mentally and spiritually guide students through a proper explanation of the Taekwon-Do philosophy. When a student is confused by a principle of Taekwon-Do, he might acquire incorrect perceptions of the Taekwon-Do philosophy. Instructing involves clarification of philosophy and facilitation of mental and spiritual growth as well as physical training.

Teaching Taekwon-Do, both technique and philosophy, requires a sufficient amount of understanding by the instructor. However, if an instructor is faced with questions from his students that are beyond his knowledge base, the honorable thing to do is to refer the students to another master or a higher-ranking teacher for an explanation. A master must have the strength of character to admit to himself and his students that no master, no school, holds all knowledge, all answers. Teachers, as well as students, should strive to refine and increase their knowledge and move developmentally ever forward, rather than rely on the glory of past achievements. One must also have sufficient knowledge of the body and its functions in order to teach Taekwon-Do. Basic knowledge of anatomy, physiology, and athletic training methods should be a requirement for a Taekwon-Do instructor, especially for the instructor who decides to open and run his own dojang.

Too often, unnecessary accidents and injuries happen in Taekwon-Do training due to a lack of understanding of movement. In modern times, being skilled at Taekwon-Do is not in and of itself enough of a foundation for teaching this art. Being a great Taekwon-Do teacher not only requires Taekwon-Do ability and skill, but also academic dedication to furthering one's education. The extent of this education depends on the level of dedication and interest the individual has in studying and improving his Taekwon-Do. The mind must be developed alongside the body. A Taekwon-Do teacher should not only be a leader in technique and physicality of movement, but also in the mental and spiritual aspects of the Taekwon-Do philosophy.

Mastery is not a single achievement; mastery is a state of being that constantly redefines itself. Without students, there is no master; there is only a great practitioner. A master needs students to identify himself as such, much like a student needs a mirror to identify and correct his stances. Without students, the art that is created through one's application of Taekwon-Do is only temporary. Through students, this art lives on. The greatest accomplishment one can achieve in Taekwon-Do is to foster students who exceed one's own skill and philosophical understanding.

V. Moral Culture

People study Taekwon-Do for a variety of reasons, but those who are truly dedicated to this art are truly dedicated to personal development. This dedication is based in the pursuit of perfection: physical as well as mental and spiritual refinement. Taekwon-Do has a strong moral culture that shapes the understanding and attitude of practitioners toward Taekwon-Do and life as a whole. The moral code of Traditional Taekwon-Do consists of a blend of multiple philosophies, which include Zen Buddhism, Confucianism, Daoism, and the code of the Hwa-Rang. The Hwa-Rang were a Buddhist elite male youth group of the Silla kingdom that lasted until the 10th century C.E. The three kingdoms—Silla, Goguryeo, and Baekje—later formed what is now known as Korea. In addition to martial training, they were educated in art, poetry, politics, and Confucianism. The Hwa-Rang had five commandments that served as a guiding ethos for living a proper life. They were:

1. Loyalty to one's lord
2. Love and respect for parents and teachers
3. Trust among friends
4. Never retreat in battle
5. Never take a life without a just cause

Similar virtues are found in other martial cultures, such as the code of conduct of the samurai, which is called the Bushido Code, and the chivalric code of medieval knights. Both of these have similar principles of ethics. Many other cultures have drawn similar conclusions about what exemplifies virtuous behavior, especially pertaining to the warrior classes. They agree that the martial artist needs wisdom in addition to martial skill; otherwise, he is merely skilled at violence. In "The Republic," Plato propagated the idea of the development of body and mind in order to generate wise leaders. Plato discussed the need for physical conditioning in order to maintain proper mental functioning; however, he never addressed martial practice directly for personal development. Taekwon-Do goes one step further in that the

Taekwon-Do master should be well developed mentally and spiritually, but also highly versed in martial skill. He should become the epitome of Plato's Philosopher Warrior, but with a spiritual aspect, as well.

Taekwon-Do sums up its moral culture in five tenets, which serve as the moral and ethical foundation for all practitioners. These five tenets form the essence of moral culture in Taekwon-Do:

1. Courtesy (Ye Ui)
2. Integrity (Yom Chi)
3. Perseverance (In Nae)
4. Self-Control (Guk Gi)
5. Indomitable Spirit (Baekjul Boolgool)

These tenets are often mentioned by teachers in the dojang and quoted in publications about Taekwon-Do. However, there is rarely in-depth discussion of these concepts. It is left to the individual student to determine the meaning of each. Further, living their true intent poses a harder task than most people realize. In many dojangs, students are required to recite the tenets before or after classes alongside a student oath. Yet merely reciting the words does not change the attitude of a practitioner. To truly follow the Do of Taekwon-Do, to dedicate oneself to it, requires change that can only come about through a thorough understanding and internalization of the tenets.

By nature, humans are resistant to change. The greatest obstacle that a practitioner faces in becoming a great martial artist, such as a Taekwon-Do master, is his own consciousness. It is comparatively easy to shape the body and obtain proficiency in Taekwon. But this does not require understanding of the Do. Adhering to the moral philosophy of the Do of Taekwon is a life-long struggle that challenges each practitioner. Every new situation encountered, both in training and in life, poses an opportunity to refine one's understanding of Do and the application of it in the moment. The five tenets of Taekwon-Do represent a guideline for virtuous living and the "right" mindset for practitioners. They form the moral foundation of this art, expressed in simple terms. Each one of the tenets stands for a separate concept, but they are interconnected with and interdependent on each other. All physical aspects of Taekwon-Do need to be understood as representations and manifestations of the mental and spiritual philosophy that is Do.

1. Courtesy (Ye Ui)

Courtesy is the most basic tenet of Taekwon-Do. Courtesy plays a vital role in martial arts, as well as Asian cultures in general. This tenet refers to the obvious outward actions of being polite and well-mannered. Additionally, the concept of courtesy has a much deeper meaning in which one engages in self-reflection and acts with humility and modesty.

Students should display courtesy right from the onset of training. For the martial artist, this means basic politeness towards all people, in and out of the dojang. This extends to being respectful towards one's entire space of existence, including respect for family and ancestors, one's homeland, all things animate and inanimate, and the culture of the land and people where one resides. Courtesy requires keeping an open heart and a curious mind, a willingness to try new experiences. Most of all, it means looking at people as people, not judging them based on race, gender, religion, or other characteristics.

In the dojang, there are set rules of appropriate behavior that practitioners abide by. Examples include bowing to the dojang when entering or leaving, and bowing to the teacher before and after class. Many dojangs have their own variations on the rules of etiquette, but the basic idea remains the same. Structured etiquette teaches students to respect the dojang and its members, but also to take a moment to become aware of their own purpose in this space. For example, bowing changes the attitude and the perspective of a practitioner. The practice of bowing can be used as a moment to return to oneself before starting or after finishing practice. With time, a Taekwon-Do practitioner should retain the same attitude towards any space that is entered, not just the dojang. Every space deserves respect and attentiveness to its purpose. The same applies to other people, and all other aspects of life.

All students in the dojang should be treated equally, disregarding race, gender, or religious views. The only acknowledged difference between students should be rank, which is meritocratic and based on one's level of skill, knowledge, and experience. Every student deserves the same amount of respect, regardless of belt level. And yet, with rank comes responsibility. More is expected of higher-ranked students with respect to courteous behavior, both for courtesy's own sake and for modeling proper behavior for lower-ranked students. While taking pride in one's achievements is understandable, this pride should be internalized; it should not be displayed to others. This exemplifies the modest and humble practitioner. It is also a form of courtesy to those of lower rank. Higher-ranking students should strive to be the epitome of courtesy, and not boast about their skills or be dismissive towards lower-ranking students.

The tenet of courtesy includes respect for oneself. These days, children are praised and rewarded for mediocre results and losses in competition. How can an achievement hold value when everything is rewarded? It is important to acknowledge children's efforts and assist their progress, but in moderation and at appropriate times. Praising success and rewarding excellence teaches children to value themselves and their work accurately, not to celebrate mediocrity. By having an accurate yardstick with which to measure their progress, children learn where they are succeeding, where they can improve, and to value the improvements they make. This engenders genuine understanding and respect for oneself and one's abilities.

The same applies to adults. Effort should be directed towards perfecting one's skill, not towards winning tournaments and trophies. Through focused training, a practitioner's skill improves. Eventually, he receives praise from peers, students, and spectators. This praise should be accepted humbly and not dwelled upon. The greatest level of self-esteem that a student can possess does not need praise from others. A student who has learned to respect himself and his own efforts, who has completely internalized the desire to train and perfect technique, is beginning to understand the Traditional Taekwon-Do philosophy of courtesy to oneself.

Courtesy to oneself and to others is reflected in the yin-yang; a student's level of courtesy affects others, who affect him in return. While his level of self-respect should not be affected by those around him, the give-and-take of respectful and polite behavior between people is impacted by the expression of one towards another. The more polite and respectful a person is to those around him, the more he receives in return. The opposite is also true; rudeness and lack of respect are reflected back upon a student who shows these characteristics.

The Taekwon-Do belt is a symbol of achievement, a representation of the hard work and persistence required to accomplish rank, and should therefore be treated with respect. Special rules of etiquette exist to show courtesy towards one's belt. It should never touch the ground. Students should not touch each other's belts. A student must show care for his belt: Keeping it knotted when not being worn symbolizes retention of the effort expended while wearing it; not washing the belt is another show of respect for the exertion put forth while training—washing it would represent washing away such effort; and always keeping it in a place of honor is a lesson in mindfulness. All the work, all the Qi that is generated through Taekwon-Do practice, is stored in the belt; it should be valued as a part of oneself and shown courtesy as a show of courtesy for oneself.

The same applies to the uniform. A student's dobok should always be clean and handled with respect. The clean, white dobok represents readiness to practice Do and the appreciation a student has for the art. It is, again, a practice in mindfulness of the things a student respects, and the act of taking responsibility for the things he owns. By doing this, a student shows courtesy for himself as well as the art.

For a teacher, courtesy means having patience and compassion for his students. The higher the level and skill of a Taekwon-Do practitioner, including masters, the more modest and humble he should be. A good teacher only cares about the progress of his students; personal agendas are left outside of the dojang. The good teacher uses his skill only to demonstrate technique to assist students in understanding Taekwon-Do, to promote the art, or to show the possibilities achievable through Taekwon-Do, never for personal glory. A true master does not need to show his skill. The only true manifestation of power is not to use it. This is a representation of courtesy to the master's abilities, and to those around him.

2. Integrity (Yom Chi)

In Taekwon-Do, integrity has a plethora of meanings. On the surface, it stands for loyalty and honesty, but it also implies doing the right thing and making the right choices. The "right thing" within the context of Taekwon-Do is acting in accordance with the Taekwon-Do philosophy. Simply put, words, deeds, and attitude need to be in harmony with each other and with Do. Integrity cannot be maintained when saying one thing and doing another; hypocrisy and integrity are not bedfellows. We are forced to live with cognitive dissonance about many things in daily life; Taekwon-Do should not be one of them.

This concept becomes increasingly important as a student progresses on to teach at his own dojang. Skill alone does not constitute a great Taekwon-Do practitioner. Often flaws in the personality of a student are overlooked because of his great talent and skill. However, his attitude, understanding of Do, and the level to which he is living Do are as important as his physical abilities. Without an understanding of Do, and the honest pursuit of living Do, Taekwon-Do is merely a skillful application and not an art. Integrity in Taekwon-Do means carrying the principles of Do into all aspects of life. Once a practitioner is fully immersed in the Taekwon-Do philosophy, it should be an inseparable part of his state of mind.

This philosophy is introduced to the beginning student through the rules of conduct in the dojang. He should be honest and sincere at all times. He should not ask for higher rank, but accept what is given to him. A teacher should not award rank to an undeserving student for personal favors or political reasons. A Taekwon-Do teacher needs to separate himself from any favoritism; if he is guided by his own biases, he will not be able to bring out the potential in all students. A teacher's passion should be only for Taekwon-Do, not for the individual person that practices it. It can be difficult for both student and master to control their emotions. However, the Taekwon-Do practitioner should not lose his temper or display his frustration if he fails a break or loses a sparring match. The Taekwon-Do teacher should not lose his temper when teaching. The Taekwon-Do philosophy underlies all of these rules of conduct; they not only teach appropriate behavior in the dojang, but also provoke thoughtfulness on the part of the practitioner, providing a path into Do.

Integrity also means showing one's best effort and giving one's complete attention in class at all times. This shows respect to the teacher and to the self, intertwining integrity with courtesy. Taekwon-Do training is a serious matter and deserves respect. A student should never try to cheat in any way, to achieve something that he does not deserve or is not ready for. Also, in traditional understanding, a student should commit himself to one style, one school, and one teacher only. Many of the modern Taekwon-Do dojangs teach an expanded curriculum to students, including other martial arts. Sometimes schools offer different martial arts from different instructors in the same dojang. This is usually done to support the commercial sustainability of the school. In these cases, the idea of staying loyal to a single art is sacrificed to ensure the survival of a school. This constitutes a conflict with the Taekwon-Do philosophy.

Every school owner has to make his own decision as to how much he wants to adhere to traditional values, and whether it is feasible for him to maintain these values. The ability to feed oneself and one's family is usually considered more important than following an ideal. However, adhering to ideals whenever possible should be a school owner's guiding principle. Integrity involves standing up for one's beliefs and not compromising just for the sake of convenience. Yet every Taekwon-Do student and master must decide for himself how much he values the Taekwon-Do philosophy, and how much he is willing to sacrifice for it. Since teaching Taekwon-Do has become a business for many instructors and their livelihood depends on it, they are constantly conflicted as they try to find the right balance between commercialization and the maintenance of values.

The level of integrity one maintains in one's life and dojang is a personal choice. Living in strict adherence to the Taekwon-Do philosophy makes life more difficult at times, and can require school owners to accept a decrease in their financial income in order to maintain the values of Traditional Taekwon-Do. Instructors are tempted by various marketing strategies and add-on programs to increase the profit margin of their schools. However, teaching Taekwon-Do should never be about profit. It is important to be able to earn a living while running a dojang, but if one considers only the profit of one's school, one has picked the wrong profession. An instructor should consider the accomplishments of his students as the measure of his own success, rather than using a financial yardstick. This is described by the Japanese word "shokunin," which describes a business owner with a conscience and awareness of social responsibility. Shokunin indicates being a master of one's profession, but also includes the concept of being socially responsible while maintaining and improving one's business. It also refers to assisting one's community by helping to improve it, rather than just profiting from it. In Taekwon-Do, this can be done in several ways, such as volunteering at community events, providing free sessions for school programs, or offering self-defense classes to the general public. Adhering to the concept of shokunin reflects on the integrity of an instructor as well as the entire school.

Being active in the community is an important part of the Taekwon-Do philosophy. The personal strength a student acquires through training should be used to help and protect those in need. Showing civility and courage in an emergency, or simply helping somebody lift a heavy object, are examples of integrity and community service. Instructors who create service opportunities for their students are giving back to the community, but are also teaching their students the concepts of integrity and compassion. However, maintaining adherence to the tenet of integrity is a constant struggle. Every situation has to be examined, and sometimes compromises need to be made. Integrity is an ideal to strive towards that poses a great challenge to all practitioners.

I recommend that at the end of each day, every practitioner take some introspective time. Not only for the sake of reflecting on techniques that he has learned, but also to recall how he handled the events of the day. How did his actions affect other people? How have words spoken and actions taken led to reactions or consequences during the day? How could altering those words and actions have led to different outcomes? Much like reflecting upon how foot placement can change body posture, or choosing a different technique while sparring, it is essential to consider the day and its events and contemplate how adjusting words and actions can produce a more contributing outcome in the future.

Integrity involves reflecting upon oneself and ensuring that no compromises were made for personal gain or mere convenience. One should always examine whether or not a decision will compromise a virtuous life and moral values. Taekwon-Do teaches personal responsibility, and in accordance with the tenet of integrity, this means bearing the consequences of one's choices. Every word spoken should be spoken with awareness and care. In Taekwon-Do a student learns that no punch can be taken back, so striking another person should be a last resort and it should only be done if it is absolutely necessary. The same applies to words. One should accept responsibility for all of one's actions, verbal and non-verbal, and not blame others for their consequences. Integrity consists of accepting one's mistakes with dignity, and remedying any damage one has caused with humility and courtesy. In Taekwon-Do, strength is not only measured in physical ability, but also in strength of character. A true master will always strive to refine both.

3. Perseverance (In Nae)

Perseverance, in simple terms, means: Never quit! In Taekwon-Do, the tenet of perseverance can be observed in many ways. A good example is breaking. When a practitioner attempts to break material with a certain technique and fails, it takes a lot of perseverance and courage to try again and again until the break is completed. It takes determination to overcome the pain of a bruised hand and the fear of experiencing more pain while continuing the break. However, once a practitioner has set out to do a certain break, the Taewkwon-Do tenet of perseverance requires that he follow through and complete it. It is considered dishonorable to give up, change the breaking technique, or reduce the amount of material that the individual is trying to break. The exception to this is when a teacher determines the break to be too risky, and instructs the student to stop or change technique in order to prevent injury. This is more common amongst lower belt ranks, who have not had the experience necessary to appropriately gauge their own skill level. An advanced practitioner has to show adequate assessment of his own ability; if he overestimates his ability, he will choose a break or an amount of material that might be too challenging to him. It is better to be modest and not risk injury than to attempt breaks that one is not ready for.

Another aspect of perseverance in Taekwon-Do is the hard work and dedication it takes for a student to progress. It requires patience and a great deal of self-motivation to refine the hyeong and curriculum techniques required for each belt level. To fortify muscle memory of the movements, helping to ensure progress, it is recommended that students practice these at home, especially if they are unable to attend classes every day. Sometimes a student will become impatient when he believes himself ready to progress to the next level, even though his teacher has told him to wait and work more. A student should realize that he is not practicing for his belt rank, but for the overall betterment of himself and his skill in Taekwon-Do. A belt is merely a representation of his efforts and experience, ability, and attitude. Each rank is a representation of the commitment and dedication that a student shows to Taekwon-Do.

Holding the rank of black belt is a lifetime commitment, and should not be taken lightly. As such, the road to black belt is paved in blood, sweat, and tears. Black belt is a rank that anyone can achieve, but only through perseverance. During his training, a student learns to overcome many obstacles in order to reach black belt. He will face discouragement from losses in sparring matches, failed breaks, bruises, scoldings from his teacher, long struggles to master techniques, lack of time for training, and/or injuries. A multitude of incidents will challenge a student's will to try again and again. Like the storm shakes the bamboo stalk, he will be rattled, both physically and mentally. But after the storm, he should lift himself up and keep going. Everybody falls, but the truly committed stand back up and continue.

Perseverance also involves learning from one's mistakes and failures, trying to always improve oneself—in Taekwon-Do as well as in life. It is erroneous to think that anyone will ever achieve absolute mastery of Taekwon-Do. A student should be wary of the pride he takes in his skill, and the arrogance that can come with such pride. The true essence of perseverance is to work constantly to approach perfection, even knowing that perfection can never truly be reached. Perseverance involves putting on dobok and belt day after day, never complaining, never showing tiredness or discomfort, and always trying harder than before. One can only work to the fullest extent of one's abilities, but first one must understand one's abilities and their limitations.

In Taekwon-Do, a student conditions his body and mind to overcome their weaknesses. Once strengthened, he can set out to achieve anything. All that is required is dedication and hard work.

Perseverance is directly linked to the tenet of indomitable spirit. They are closely related, and one cannot exist without the other. Perseverance is the practice of indomitable spirit. Life can be challenging at times. People are discouraging and mean towards each other, sometimes for no obvious reason. There is no guarantee that one's hard work will be rewarded in the long run, but to persevere is to continue trying. Even if the desired result does not occur, one learns more about oneself in the process, and refines who one is. In Taekwon-Do, this is all that matters. How long, how much, and how well can one practice Taekwon-Do? How close to perfection can one take this art? These answers are to be found within each individual. To persevere means to never give up, to try again and again, regardless of the end result.

4. Self-Control (Guk Gi)

Aside from courtesy, self-control is the most visible tenet in Taekwon-Do. It is a skill practiced and learned every time a student attends class. It begins by learning to stand at attention without fidgeting. First, students learn to control their bodies, and later, their minds. Physical discipline leads to mental discipline. Controlling one's impulses, inhibitions, emotions, and desires is a skill that is polished over the course of a lifetime. Learning to control the body and movement of the limbs is fairly easy compared to learning to control one's internal drives. For example, watching a precise execution of ilbo taeryon is fascinating; however, the intangible, the internal control of impulses and emotions, is a much greater achievement. By nature, we are driven by our impulses. The untrained mind is much more susceptible to the whims of emotional or physical needs than the trained mind. It takes training to overcome hunger, thirst, tiredness, soreness, or any other physical state of being and to exert one's will over the body. But it takes even more training to resist the impulse to follow one's desires or temptations.

If one has no discipline over the mind, one can never be truly immersed in Taekwon-Do. One's choices will be tainted by desires that lead away from the Taekwon-Do philosophy. A Taekwon-Do master should have control over himself at all times and not be compromised by temptation. In Taekwon-Do, self-control is visible through physical feats, but the unseen, and more valuable, aspect of self-control involves controlling one's temper, having patience, bearing frustration, and accepting criticism. In Taekwon-Do, one should never lose control over one's feelings. In sparring and other partner exercises, this can and will lead to injury. A practitioner who loses his temper in sparring matches will not only be defeated by his opponent, but also increases the risk of injury to himself and his partner. The same risk of injury follows for all physical movement, as well as mental activity. Therefore, in Taekwon-Do, students try to maintain the state of mushin at all times. Ideally, a practitioner brings this state into his life outside of the dojang, as well, as losing control over his feelings in other areas of life also leads to conflict.

Control of oneself is essential. Being able to retract an arm or leg at the right moment so another person does not get hit, or hitting a board in the right spot so the fingers of the board holders do not get bruised, are examples of physical self-control. In Taekwon-Do, a student learns quickly that a punch or a kick can never be taken back, and an apology does not change the effects of his strikes. This is the reason why only boards are broken and no contact is made during sparring. In Taekwon-Do, as in life, we need to choose our words and actions wisely. Self-control includes awareness and mindfulness of one's space of existence. Again, an apology will not change any events that have passed, or the effects they created. It is better not to be in the position of having to apologize in the first place.

Being in control of oneself means having awareness of one's thoughts, and every word is spoken with great care. As humans, we are bound to make mistakes, but we must strive to learn from them and avoid making the same mistake twice. Breaking one's hand while attempting a break should teach the practitioner to alter his technique and train more, so he can execute the break better the next time. In life, not all of our decisions have consequences as drastic as this. Still, interactions with others follow the same principle. If one's tone of voice is harsh and one's words are rude, one will alienate others.

Self-control means managing emotions such as anger and speaking and acting from a place of clarity. In the heat of the moment, one might be tempted to respond in a way that could lead to future trouble. Sparring gives a clear physical example of this. If a student accidentally makes contact due to lack of skill, his partner should not strike him back. Instead the partner should strive to position himself better and react faster the next time.

However, a practitioner should be able to control his movements to the point where there is no unwanted contact with his partner. A high-quality movement is a movement that can be stopped and reversed at any time during its execution. A skilled Taekwon-Do practitioner should not only be able to execute high-quality movements, but also have the ability to redirect any movement at any given time. This level of self-control requires intensive training, total presence of body and mind, and awareness of all movement. Self-control in Taekwon-Do requires presence within oneself; it also involves living in the moment. If the mind of the practitioner is preoccupied with other events, he will pose a risk to his fellow students. After a certain stage of training, injuries happen solely because of a lack of presence. In life, one should always try to be present in the moment and not live in the future or the past. The only time that one can directly affect is the existing moment. Taekwon-Do teaches this principle so that a student learns to be present within himself and focus on each move. Since the present is in constant motion, he should be, too. A master is only as good as his current move, and he should always attempt to make the next one better than the last one.

5. Indomitable Spirit (Baekjul Boolgool)

Throughout history there have been many recorded feats of extraordinary resilience and fighting spirit against an overwhelming force. Leonidas and his 300 is one example. His conviction and love for his country and people helped fend off the Persians. Many of the Taekwon-Do hyeong refer to historical figures in Korean history who fought and died for their country, overcame great obstacles, and dedicated their lives to an ideal. We all possess the potential for such spirit, which is rooted in passion. It is the driving force behind putting on one's dobok every day, practicing hyeong over and over again, and standing up and trying again after falling over or being defeated.

Through Taekwon-Do training, one's spirit and mental fortitude grow. A Taekwon-Do student learns to never give up and to find a way to turn a negative into a positive, even if the odds are seemingly against him. Indomitable spirit is reflected in one's passion, courage, and resilience; it is the intangible, internal force that is demonstrated through the practical application of perseverance. Without passion, there is no motivation to persevere, to strive, to struggle to achieve greatness. Passion for Taekwon-Do gives one the strength to continue after an injury, or to manage physical pain and keep on going. Yet it is much more than mere passion that has been sparked once a practitioner dedicates himself to the Taekwon-Do philosophy. Taekwon-Do is a way of life, a commitment to the art and to oneself.

This spark of passion, this internal spirit, drives one to overcome any obstacle that might stand in one's way. It inspires students to fight prejudice, discouragement, and austerity with a smile on their faces, and to keep moving forward. Taekwon-Do should come from the heart and the soul. In life, there is nothing that cannot be achieved if spirit, soul, and passion are committed to accomplishing it. No matter how long it takes to reach that goal, the dedicated practitioner will find the strength to pursue it. In Taekwon-Do, the initial goal is to achieve 1st Dan. But this is where the true journey starts. A black belt is just the first step on a student's journey in Do. When a student reaches black belt, he has made the commitment to dedicate himself to the art.

The bamboo plant is a common and apt symbol for the tenets of Taekown-Do. Bamboo is hollow inside, but the nodes are strong. It grows only in one direction, but is not rigid; it is flexible and can sway with the wind, surviving turbulence without breaking. These characteristics are synonymous with aspects of the Taekwon-Do philosophy and, as such, live bamboo plants and artwork depicting bamboo are traditional gifts to the master of a newly opened dojang.

Bamboo represents straightforwardness and clarity of mind as it grows only in one direction. This is also representative of loyalty and dedication to one path or one master, which reflect the virtues of courtesy and integrity. Living a virtuous, simple, and modest life is another virtue identified with this plant, as bamboo does not bear flowers or fruit. This lack of self-aggrandizement is reflective of both courtesy and self-control. Bamboo also symbolizes steadfastness, perseverance, and indomitable spirit, as it bends during the storm, but stands upright after the wind has quieted down, and because it is a plant that grows in all seasons while retaining its leaves.

One of the most important symbolic meanings of bamboo is the hollowness of its stalks. The aspect of emptiness or hollowness is a recurring theme in martial arts. Rooted in Buddhism, it refers to the Buddhist dogma that attempts detachment from the illusions of the world. Desire creates suffering, and the martial artist should strive to free himself of worldly desires and their control over him. Buddhist dogma suggests following the Eightfold Path that was laid out by Siddhartha Gautama to end suffering for the individual. The Eightfold Path leads to understanding the true nature of all things and leads to reaching a higher state of existence, that of enlightenment and, ultimately, access to Nirvana. Nirvana is salvation from the circle of death and rebirth and the chains of karma. Living plants and artistic representations of bamboo remind a practitioner to strive for the emptiness of its stalks, as this will put him on the path to Nirvana. Taekwon-Do does not promote a religious affiliation of any sort, but it retains the ideal of freeing oneself from the oppression of attachment and worldly desire.

Victory offers an excellent example of a worldly desire. In Taekwon-Do, it is represented by tournaments and the need to defeat another person in order to win accolades and awards. This is contrary to the core philosophy of Taekwon-Do. Competitions have benefits for participants, and there are many arguments that support participation in them. However, the need to triumph over another person, to be recognized by others as the superior practitioner, creates attachment to values which guide practitioners away from the original purpose of the art.

Taekwon-Do should be practiced for the refinement of self, not for comparison between one's strength and skill and that of others. To rid oneself of worldly attachments and desires is the central aspect of Buddhism, especially Zen Buddhism. In Taekwon-Do, this concept manifests itself through daily training of the body to gain control over oneself and one's passions. The five tenets facilitate this philosophical goal.

Though it shares Buddhist moral values, Taekwon-Do philosophy does not embody any religious practice, nor require adherence to Buddhism or any other religion. However, Zen Buddhist ideas are found in Taekwon-Do philosophy, and knowledge of their origins is helpful in understanding Taekwon-Do and for enhancing a practitioner's personal development.

VI. Spiritual Aspects

Taekwon-Do teaches the facilitation of a state of harmony and balance within the practitioner. Through individual transformation, Taekwon-Do provides a path to creating a more peaceful world. The body becomes a vessel, a tool for spiritual development. As the spirit of a practitioner is developed and refined, his internal and external conflicts recede in frequency and intensity and constructive resolutions are sought out and implemented. Further, a practitioner's focus moves from self to community, engendering engagement in service opportunities and mutually beneficial support networks. Additionally, positive role modeling can inspire others to act in similar ways. By reducing participatory negativity and increasing the input of positive energy, the overall level of strife in the world ebbs.

In practice, however, too much emphasis has been put on the development of the body and techniques of Taekwon-Do, rather than the practice of Do. Do is intangible; to discuss it only as an intellectual exercise is a limiting endeavor since it needs to be lived and practiced to be truly understood. In daily Taekwon-Do practice, Do is rarely addressed, and teachers only hint at explanations of it. This is because Do needs to be experienced through constant practice and adherence to the moral culture of Taekwon-Do. It also requires personal reflection by practitioners. A student should ask himself every day what he has learned, and how deep his understanding of Do has become. Do is literally a "way," a lifestyle, a commitment to the pursuit of excellence in all aspects of life. The visible, physical expression of Taekwon-Do is merely the manifestation of an individual's Do.

In his book "Zen Art of Self Defense" Grandmaster Kwon Jae Hwa refers to the Do of Taekwon-Do as one of the paths to reach satori. It facilitates the state of emptiness and insight into the true nature of being, thus ending the karmic circle. Taekwon-Do has its philosophical foundations in the teachings of Zen Buddhism, which is not well understood by many Westerners. The idea of self-cultivation to improve all aspects of life is found in Western philosophies, though presentation of the concept and implementation differs from Eastern traditions. Finding access to the Korean roots, the culture in which Taekwon-Do is based, might pose difficulties for Westerners. Each practitioner must find similar values and modalities of thinking between Korean culture and his own roots in order to fully understand and live the Taekwon-Do philosophy. There is no need to look outside of oneself or one's culture to find explanations for Do, as many cultures contain within them similar values and ideals; it is merely a matter of making connections between cultures.

The concept of emptiness, the state of satori, can be experienced by a Taekwon-Do practitioner even if he is not aware of the existence of the concept of satori. Taekwon-Do students are not asked to convert to Buddhism or follow any other religious practice. In fact, Taekwon-Do should be free of any bias that might exclude people on a discriminatory basis. Understanding Taekwon-Do as a spiritual path and as a way of life is a choice that each individual has to make for himself. Most practitioners never acknowledge Taekwon-Do as a spiritual path and only focus on its practice. However, developing physical skill and gaining control over one's body to the point where great physical feats can be achieved is the first step on the path to Do.

Taekwon-Do provides a system, a modality to develop one's body, mind, and spirit, and it should be regarded as this: a modality. It can be transcended to affect all other aspects of life. In the practice of this art, a student has to realize that, simultaneously, all is Taekwon-Do, and yet nothing is. Taekwon-Do in itself is an idea, a concept that comes to life only through the performance of it. The same applies to its philosophy. As a practitioner's consciousness dictates his patterns of movement, thoughts, concepts, and interpretations of reality, he shapes and gives Taekwon-Do form.

A dedicated student believes in the ability to become a skilled and powerful Taekwon-Do practitioner. However, this belief can become overpowering, causing the student to forget that he is not one thing, but many; such a practitioner focuses solely on the physical, disregarding the mental and spiritual aspects of Taekwon-Do. Becoming a skilled practitioner is the level where most Taekwon-Do students become stuck. They do not transcend the physical aspect of Taekwon-Do; they fail to balance out their practice with mental and spiritual growth. Like standing only on one leg, it leads to imbalance in mind, body, and spirit. When practicing Taekwon-Do, one should seek to balance all three aspects, which should also carry over into daily life. Taekwon-Do creates peace and harmony within a practitioner as he becomes aware of himself as a whole being, though these states vary with each individual. Peace is not static, nor is harmony; they are fluid states in constant motion that a practitioner must actively keep balanced.

A Taekwon-Do student learns to adapt and respond appropriately to new situations and to different opinions that he is confronted with, and solves them in a calm and adequate manner. Peacefulness through Taekwon-Do is created by abiding by the tenets of Taekwon-Do, striving to live a virtuous life, and being a contributing member of one's society. The measure of a successful Taekwon-Do student is not how high he can kick or how many boards he can break; it is the possession of the confidence and skills to make the right choices and promote justice. Without this strength, he becomes a victim to the arbitrariness of others. Through Taekwon-Do, a student learns to overcome his fears and gain control over himself. As most conflicts are sparked by fear, this education reduces the frequency of conflict in his life and provides conflict-management abilities for those situations which are unavoidable.

To understand oneself is to understand one's own humanity, which allows for an understanding of the humanity of all people. Through this new perspective, a student begins to see himself as a part of the collective human race, rather than as an isolated individual or as part of a culture separate from others. Peace involves respecting others' opinions, and debating with reason, not with force. Traditional Taekwon-Do teaches a student to use force only to defend himself or those in need. Force cannot be used to convince others of one's opinions. Through Taekwon-Do study, a student comes to realize that his actions can cause suffering in others. A practitioner's technique will cause injury to himself or to others if he has no control over it. The same applies to his words. If he is not aware and mindful of his words, he might hurt others with them. A practitioner comes to this realization as he struggles through the various stages of Taekwon-Do training, the agonizing pain of an injury, and the mental anguish of persevering until a difficult curriculum has been mastered. These experiences permit the practitioner to see his actions and words in a new light; by coming to appreciate the depth, breadth, and negativity of physical and verbal abuse, he will strive to put an end to it for himself and others.

In Zen, a state of "emptiness" is sought by its practitioners. The term "fullness" describes this better. Fullness includes everything that exists in one's space of existence. Awareness of this could be called the "awakened self" or the "aware self." This is a different perspective on the Zen concept. Rather than excluding, trying to rise above or to let go of one's impulses, thoughts, and feelings, one embraces them. Existence no longer controls the student; rather, the student manages his existence.

To achieve this, a student has to encounter himself and face who he truly is. First, he struggles with controlling his body, then he struggles with managing his emotions. In the end, he realizes that in Taekwon-Do, as well as all other realms of his existence, his biggest adversary is himself. The more powerful one becomes as a human being, the more powerful one's nemesis becomes. Dealing with personal fears and resistances poses a great challenge, and the greater the resistance to a particular thing, the greater the reward for overcoming it. The challenge of bettering oneself is worth the effort involved.

The concept most central to Hawaiian culture is 'Ohana (family). Family in Hawaii includes much more than blood relations. It involves a wide network of people lending each other mutual support. 'Ohana cares for all members of this network and achieves great things when the entire family works together. This is an excellent allegory for the individual self. Encountering all aspects of oneself and embracing them with compassion creates a network, an 'Ohana, within; there is no internal resistance to what the individual aspires to achieve. When an individual acknowledges all aspects of himself, he is able to manage them rather than allowing them to control him. It is, in essence, the same goal as achieving satori through Zen. However, looking at oneself as a family unit is an inclusive concept of achieving this state, rather than the exclusive concept of emptiness espoused in Buddhism. One understands the nature of things through understanding oneself, and therefore understands the self to be part of everything else.

As a student masters all external movement and technique, he needs to look at mastering all internal movements as well. Awareness of his inner movements, his thoughts, emotions, and personality, begins this journey. Once he encounters his true self, once he becomes aware of and gains mastery over these internal processes, he will be able to move physically and mentally without resistance. Recognition of the nature of self, acknowledgment that includes everything the self is comprised of—the good, the bad, and the ugly—allows for transcendence to an enhanced state of being. For example, if one has tight muscles in one area of one's body, one's movements will be hindered. The same applies to one's mind. If one's emotions are unsettled, one will not be able to make clear and quick decisions. Once a practitioner drops all resistance, both physically and mentally, he is free to achieve whatever he puts his mind to. This is not "mind over matter." It would be more accurate to describe it as being one with mind and matter, thus being able to alter one's physicality through altering one's consciousness as well as altering one's consciousness through altering one's physicality. This symbiotic relationship, this balance, is what Taekwon-Do strives to achieve in its practitioners.

Yet Taekwon-Do practice does not directly address dealing with one's internal self. It is a process of self-reflection that happens over time and only through a gradual progression and increased awareness of self. Looking into one's self and pursuing Taekwon-Do to the degree of mastering one's consciousness is a personal choice. Not every practitioner chooses this route. However, those who do find deep satisfaction in this decision.

Taekwon-Do offers the possibility of becoming an empowered human being, and a human being with genuine personal freedom. The degree of empowerment and freedom garnered through Taekwon-Do is a function of the extent to which a practitioner accepts Taekwon-Do as a spiritual path. The dedication with which one follows this path can only be determined by the individual practitioner. A committed Taekwon-Do practitioner gains control over his body and his mind. He has the power to choose his actions freely and not to be a slave to his own desires. This involves an awareness of the responsibility that comes with power; a devoted practitioner accepts this responsibility with forethought and care. Taekwon-Do can generate a truly free state of being where dependency and suffering become choices, rather than controlling factors in one's life.

To those not versed in Taekwon-Do philosophy, it appears that Taekwon-Do only produces the ability to exert one's will over one's body. In actuality, once a practitioner achieves mastery, every movement is an expression of being one with oneself. Every movement becomes spontaneous and voluntary, with the full support of one's entire being. This is a concept called "subtle mass," which describes the awareness and inclusion of all aspects of self. Once he accrues subtle mass and is able to harness and focus it, an individual is able to achieve great things. In Taekwon-Do, this is most commonly manifested through breaking. However, this state permeates all other areas of life. Achieving subtle mass, obtaining the support of one's entire self, allows for a truly free and empowered state of being.

In addition to the personal and spiritual development a Taekwon-Do student undergoes during his studies, Taekwon-Do creates something else of great value to the individual: It creates purpose through art. Stripping away the religious and spiritual connotations of the Taekwon-Do philosophy leaves a foundation of moral behavior through the education of body and mind. To strive to better oneself is purpose in itself. Teaching Taekwon-Do gives an instructor's existence purpose. It is the duty of a master to provide his students with an answer to the question of existence, a reason to continue to strive, practice, and refine the art. It is up to a master to provide meaning, to provide hope for students. The practice of this art becomes the reason to cope with the emptiness of oneself, the emptiness of existence, to amass as many experiences as possible, to achieve greatness on one's path beyond personal gain. The pursuit of this art constitutes purpose for the individual. When there is nothing to hold on to, moving one's body, creating art through movement, fills that void, fills the need for justification of one's existence. The art of Taekwon-Do provides hope, inspiration, and meaning for practitioners. Through this art, others are inspired, and through teaching, a master passes the art on and generates a legacy. Taekwon-Do prepares the body, mind, and spirit to be ready in the event of a physical altercation, but much more than that, it prepares the soul to cope with existence. Traditional Taekwon-Do is many things, but it is not a martial sport, it is a martial art. Taekwon-Do is only as good as the individual practicing it; with dedication and perseverance, great art and purpose can be created to solve the great questions in life.

It is rewarding for each practitioner to attempt, for both himself and the art, to reach perfection. In Taekwon-Do, each moment is celebrated through the creation of art and Do. Taekwon-Do teaches us to live life with awareness and appreciation.

Afterword

For me, Taekwon-Do is an intensely personal experience. Its practice and philosophy are in constant flux as times, people, and attitudes change. At this point in history, we are faced with different problems and challenges than when Taekwon-Do was founded in 1955. Modern technology allows for easier and faster access to shared information. Techniques are easily available through modern social media; this global sharing has evolved Taekwon-Do tremendously since I started studying it. Our value systems, lifestyles, and the geographic locations of those studying Taekwon-Do have changed as well. As such, it no longer feels necessary to fear an unprovoked assault at any given moment. Furthermore, school owners no longer challenge each other to prove the supremacy of their style or dojang.

Rather than learning hand-to-hand combat in order to defend a country, the study of Taekwon-Do has shifted focus to an individual's own progress. We can now focus on the evolution and development of ourselves physically, mentally, and spiritually. This newer goal of maintaining this incredibly fulfilling martial art for health as well as philosophical reasons creates that which is my passion. Taekwon-Do, for me, is alive and evolving; I will continue to contribute to this art, sharing it with as many practitioners as possible.

To reach Master Ippen for advice or to take classes with him, please contact:
www.taekwondohonolulu.com
david.ippen@taekwondohonolulu.com

Recommended reading

Stuart Anslow, *From Creation to Unification. The Complete Histories Behind the Ch'ang Hon Patterns*, Ireland 2013

"The Feldenkrais Method at a Glance," in: Thomas Claire, *Bodywork. What Type of Massage to Get – and How to Make the Most of It*, Laguna Beach 2006

Confucius, *The Analects*, various editions

Moshe Feldenkrais, *The Potent Self. A Study of Spontaneity and Compulsion*, Berkeley 2002

Gichin Funakoshi, *Karate-Do. My Way of Life*, New York 1975, 2013

Alex Gillis, *A Killing Art, The Untold History of Tae Kwon Do*, Toronto 2011

Peter Haskel, *Sword of Zen. Master Takuan and his Writings on the Immovable Wisdom and the Sword Taie*, University of Hawaii Press 2013

Martin Heidegger, *Introduction to Metaphysics*, Yale University Press 2014

General Choi Hong Hi, *Taekwon-Do. The Art of Self-Defence*, Sprendlingen 1994

Kwon Jae Hwa, *Zen and the Art of Self-Defense*, Munich 1971

Samy Molcho, *Body Speech*, Saint Martin's Press 1985

Yagyu Munenori, *The Life Giving Sword. Secret Teachings from the House of the Shogun*, Boston/London 2012

Miyamoto Musashi, *Book of Five Rings*, trans. Stephen F. Kaufman, Tokyo 1994

Plato, *The Republic*, various editions

Young-Chan Ro, *The Korean Neo-Confucianism of Yi Yulgok*, Albany 1989

Takuan Soho, *Tao Te Ching. Zen Teachings on the Taoist Classic*, trans. Thomas Cleary, Boston 2010

Takuan Soho, *The Unfettered Mind. Writings from Zen Master to a Master Swordsman*, Boston 2012

Daisetz Teitaro Suzuki, *An Introduction to Zen Buddhism*, New York 1964

Lao Tzu, *Tao Te Ching. An Illustrated Journey*, trans. Stephen Mitchell, London 1999, 2013

Tsunemoto Yamamoto, *Bushido. The Way of the Samurai*, ed. Justin F. Stone, original translation by Minoru Tanaka, New York 2001

Samguk Yusa, *Legends and History of the Three Kingdoms of Ancient Korea*, trans. Ha Tae-Hung and Crafton K. Mintz, 2006